Jewel this way

Transcribed by Danny Begelman

Project Manager: Jeannette DeLisa
Music Editor: Colgan Bryan
Book Art Layout: Olivia D. Novak

Album Artwork © 2001 Atlantic Recording Corporation
Album Art Direction and Design: Chad Farmer/The Lambesis Agency
Photography: Ellen von Unwerth

WARNER BROS. PUBLICATIONS
Warner Music Group
An AOL Time Warner Company
USA: 15800 NW 48th Avenue, Miami, FL 33014

WARNER/CHAPPELL MUSIC

CANADA: 15800 N.W. 48th AVENUE
MIAMI, FLORIDA 33014
SCANDINAVIA: P.O. BOX 533, VENDEVAGEN 85 B
S-182 15, DANDERYD, SWEDEN
AUSTRALIA: P.O. BOX 353
3 TALAVERA ROAD, NORTH RYDE N.S.W. 2113
ASIA: THE PENINSULA OFFICE TOWER, 12th FLOOR
18 MIDDLE ROAD
TSIM SHA TSUI, KOWLOON, HONG KONG

Carisch
NUOVA CARISCH

ITALY: VIA CAMPANIA, 12
20098 S. GIULIANO MILANESE (MI)
ZONA INDUSTRIALE SESTO ULTERIANO
SPAIN: MAGALLANES, 25
28015 MADRID
FRANCE: CARISCH MUSICOM,
25, RUE D'HAUTEVILLE, 75010 PARIS

IMP
INTERNATIONAL MUSIC PUBLICATIONS LIMITED

ENGLAND: GRIFFIN HOUSE,
161 HAMMERSMITH ROAD, LONDON W6 8BS
GERMANY: MARSTALLSTR. 8, D-80539 MUNCHEN
DENMARK: DANMUSIK, VOGNMAGERGADE 7
DK 1120 KOBENHAVNK

CONTENTS

STANDING STILL

Words by
JEWEL KILCHER
Music by
JEWEL KILCHER and RICK NOWELS

1. Cut - ting through the dark - est night are my two head - lights. Try to
2. *See additional lyrics*

keep it clear, but I'm los - ing it here to the twi - light. There's a

dead end to my left, there's a burn - ing bush to my right. You

are - n't in sight, you are - n't in sight.

Standing Still - 3 - 2
0643B

Verse 2:
Mothers on the stoop,
Boys in souped-up coupes
On this hot summer night.
Between fight and flight
Is the blind man's sight
And a choice that's right.
I roll the window down,
Feel like I'm gonna drown
In this strange town.
Feel broken down,
Feel broken down.
(To Chorus:)

JESUS LOVES YOU

Words and Music by
JEWEL KILCHER

Moderately ♩ = 80

Intro:

Verse:

Cont. rhy. simile

1. They say that Je - sus loves__ you,
   ta - tas on the TV is o - kay,
   a - bor - tion will send you

what a - bout me?__ They
I wan - na be o - kay, too.__ Hav - ing my
straight to a fi - er - y hell.__ That

say that mon - ey breaks__ you, I still wan - na see.__
pic - ture in a mag - a - zine makes me spe - cial, how spe - cial are you?__
is if the fan - at - ics don't beat Sa - tan to the kill.__

They say that you're on - ly half a - live__
They say if I do - nate e - ven I__ can
It's not what I can do for an - y - bod - y, it's

Chorus:

till you give ex - tra white - ning a__ try.
buy a lot in heav - en be - fore I__ die. } Well, I wan - na see,__
what their bod - y can do for me.

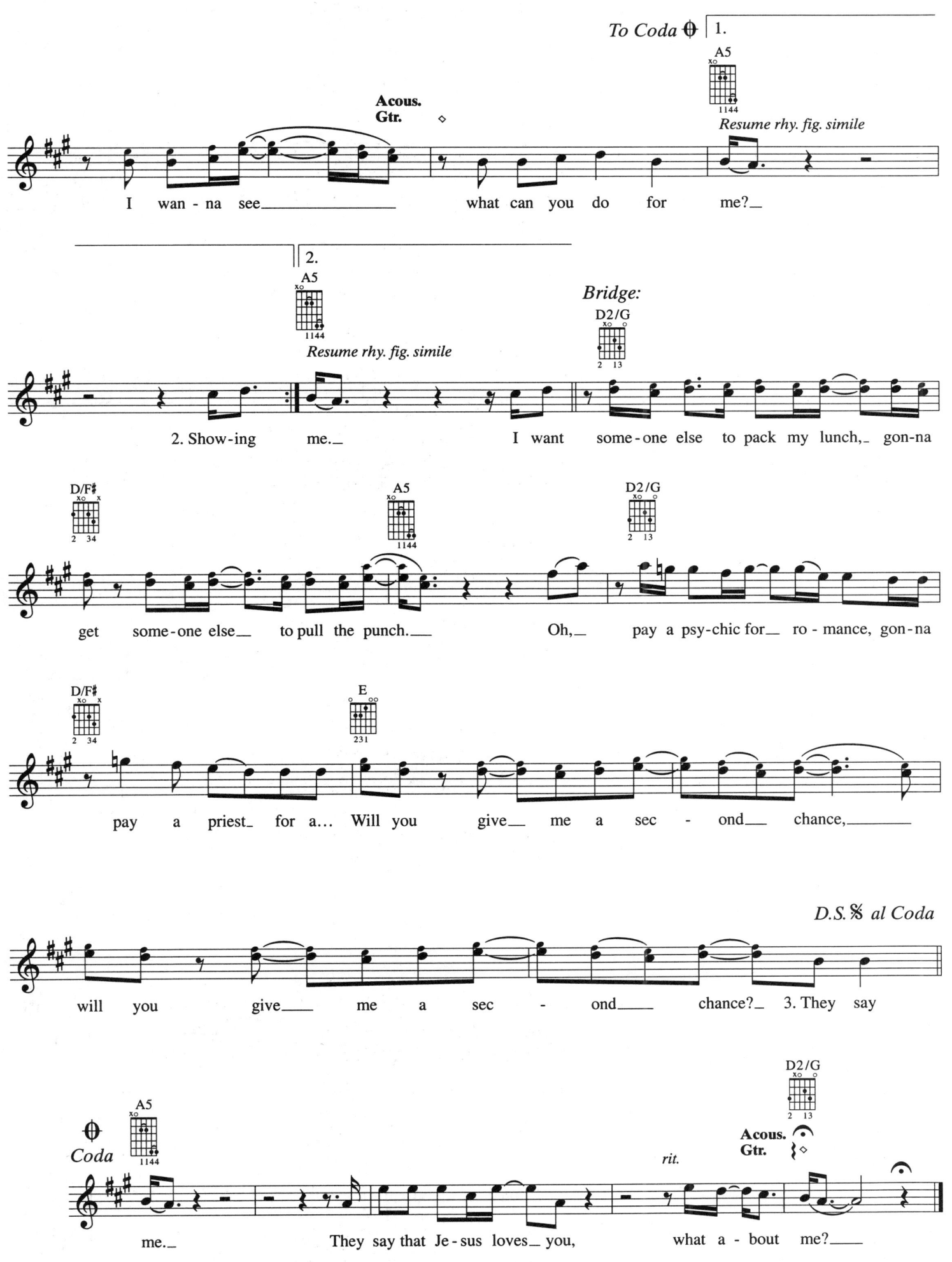

EVERYBODY NEEDS SOMEONE SOMETIME

Words and Music by
JEWEL KILCHER

1. Mar-y heard boys___ talk-in' in voic-es low,___ said she
2. Spi-vey Leeks was a drip of a man,___ he
3. Sis-ter Mar-y used to be a nun,___ she

were-n't no spring___ chick-en like she did-n't al-read-y know.___ So she
looked like a po-ta-to shoved in-to jeans.___ She
thought that she'd re-tire, and have her some fun.___

called up Jack___ from a few years back.___ She
He rec-ol-lects it was-n't that long a-go___ that he could
Mis-ter Joe (of the Phil-a-del-phi-a Joes,) well, he

Everybody Needs Someone Sometime - 4 - 1
0643B

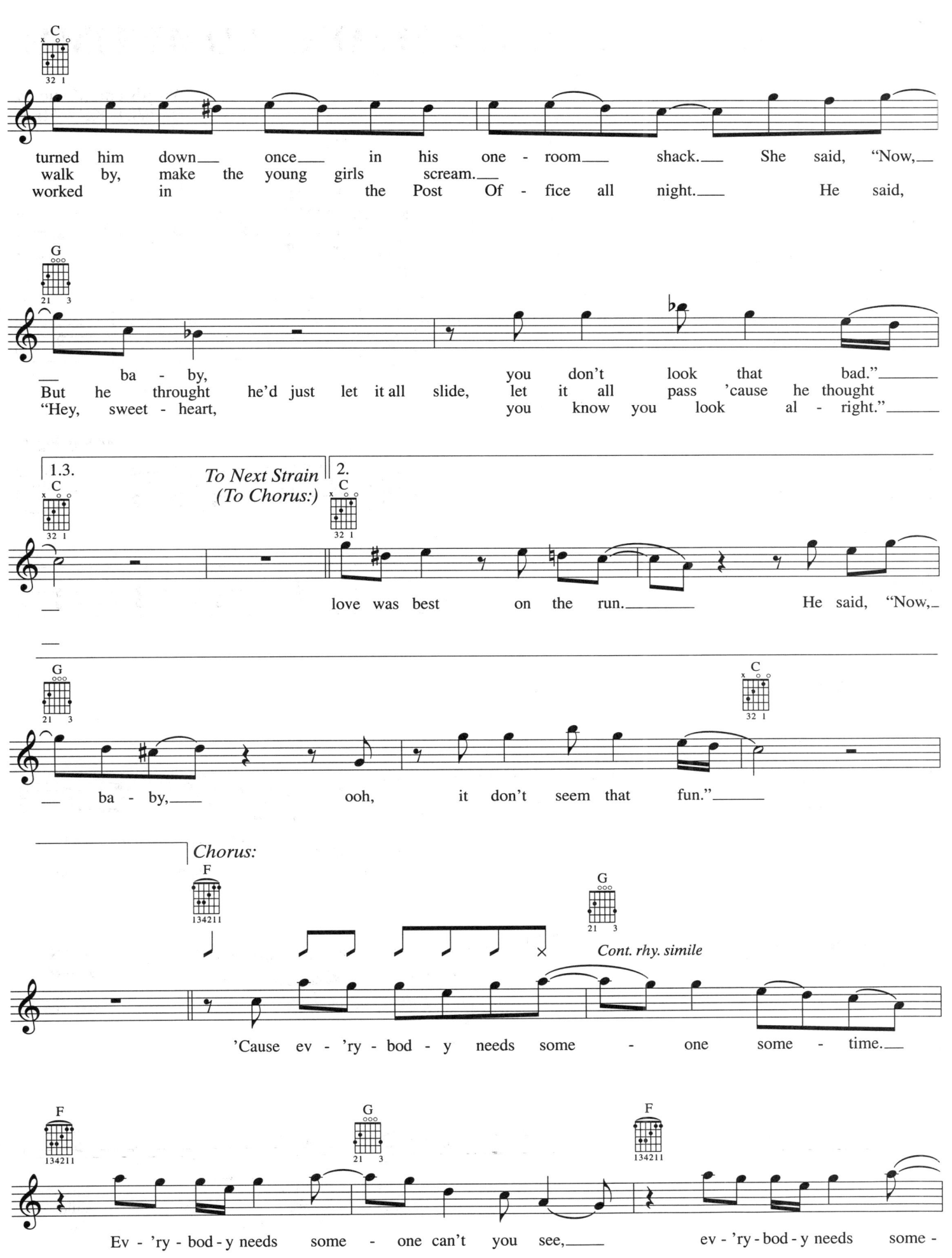

turned him down___ once___ in his one - room___ shack.___ She said, "Now,___
walk by, make the young girls scream.___
worked in the Post Of - fice all night.___ He said,

___ ba - by, you don't look that bad."___
But he throught he'd just let it all slide, let it all pass 'cause he thought
"Hey, sweet - heart, you know you look al - right."___

1.3. *To Next Strain* **2.**
(*To Chorus:*)

___ love was best on the run.___ He said, "Now,___

___ ba - by,___ ooh, it don't seem that fun."___

Chorus:

Cont. rhy. simile

'Cause ev - 'ry - bod - y needs some - one some - time.___

Ev - 'ry - bod - y needs some - one can't you see,___ ev - 'ry - bod - y needs some -

12

To Coda ⊕ | 1.

Acous. Gtr.

- one some - time._____

w/Rhy. Fig. 1 *(Elec. Gtr.), simile*

2.

Bridge:

Acous. Gtr.

Resume rhy. fig. simile

time._____ Hey there,__ hon - ey - bee,__

__ will you__ give__ me sug - ar. And if you

shake real cute I might give you_____ some

sug - ar. I was do - in' al - right on my__ own, but

Everybody Needs Someone Sometime - 4 - 3
0643B

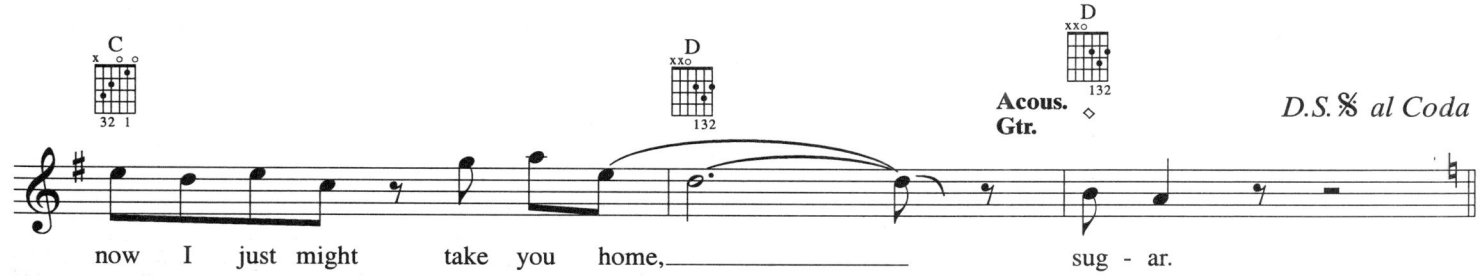

now I just might take you home,＿＿＿＿ sug - ar.

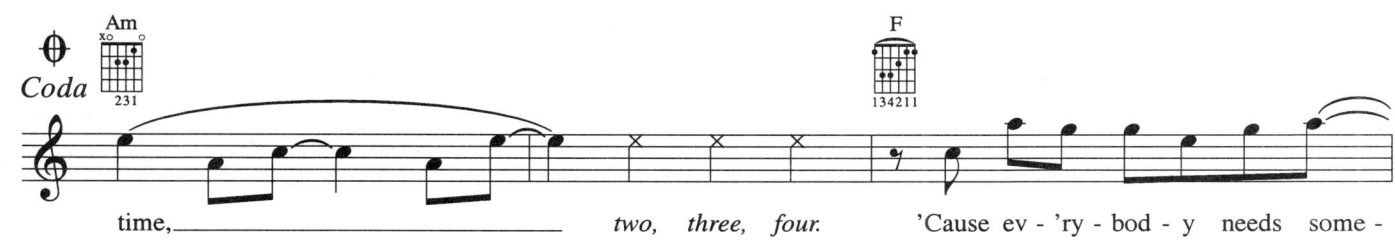

Coda

time,＿＿＿＿＿＿ *two, three, four.* 'Cause ev - 'ry - bod - y needs some -

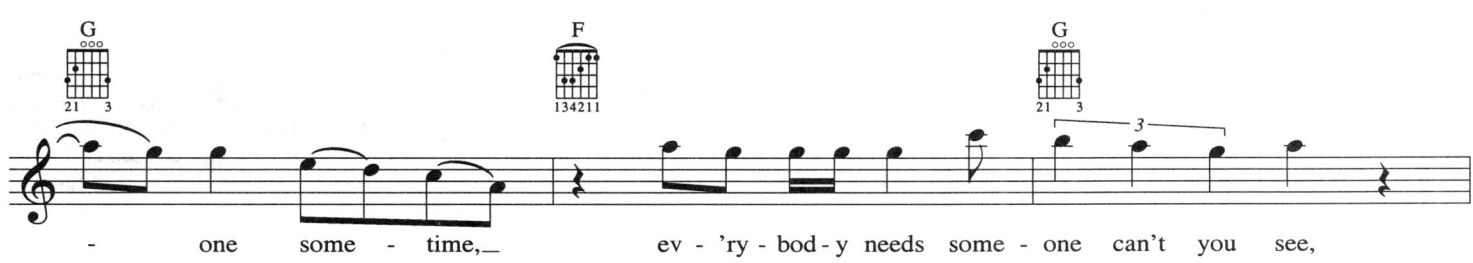

- one some - time,＿ ev - 'ry - bod - y needs some - one can't you see,

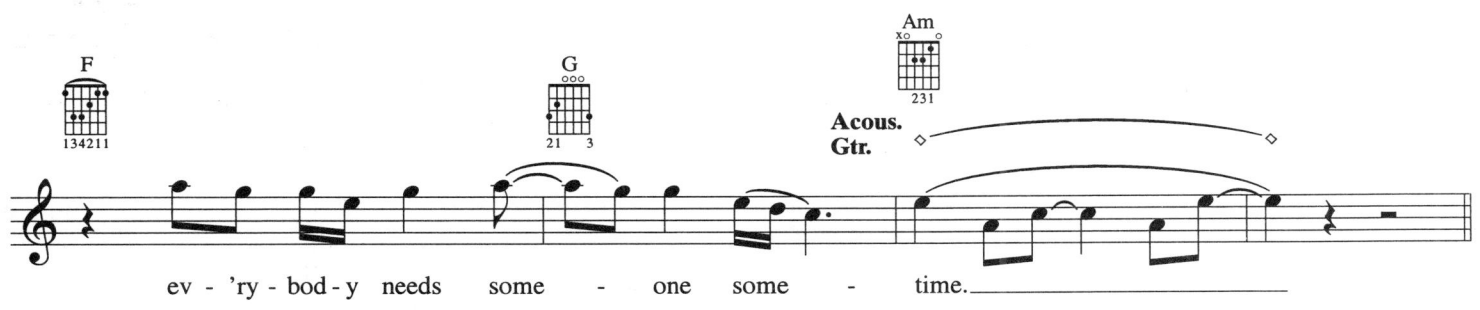

ev - 'ry - bod - y needs some - one some - time.＿＿＿＿

Outro: w/ad lib. vocal

Resume rhy. fig. simile

Ev - 'ry - bod - y needs some - one some - time.＿＿ Oh, yeah.＿

Everybody Needs Someone Sometime - 4 - 4
0643B

BREAK ME

Acous. Gtr. w/capo I

Words and Music by
JEWEL KILCHER

Moderately slow ♩ = 69
Intro:

*Suggested frames till gtr. enters at Verse.

I will meet you in some place where the light lends it-self to soft re-pose. I will let you un-dress me, but I warn you I have thorns like an-y rose.

Verses 2 & 3:

2. And you could hurt me with your bare hands,
3. Feels like be-ing un-der-wa-ter

Acous. Gtr.
capo I
Rhy. Fig. 1
mf
hold throughout

Break Me - 3 - 1
0643B

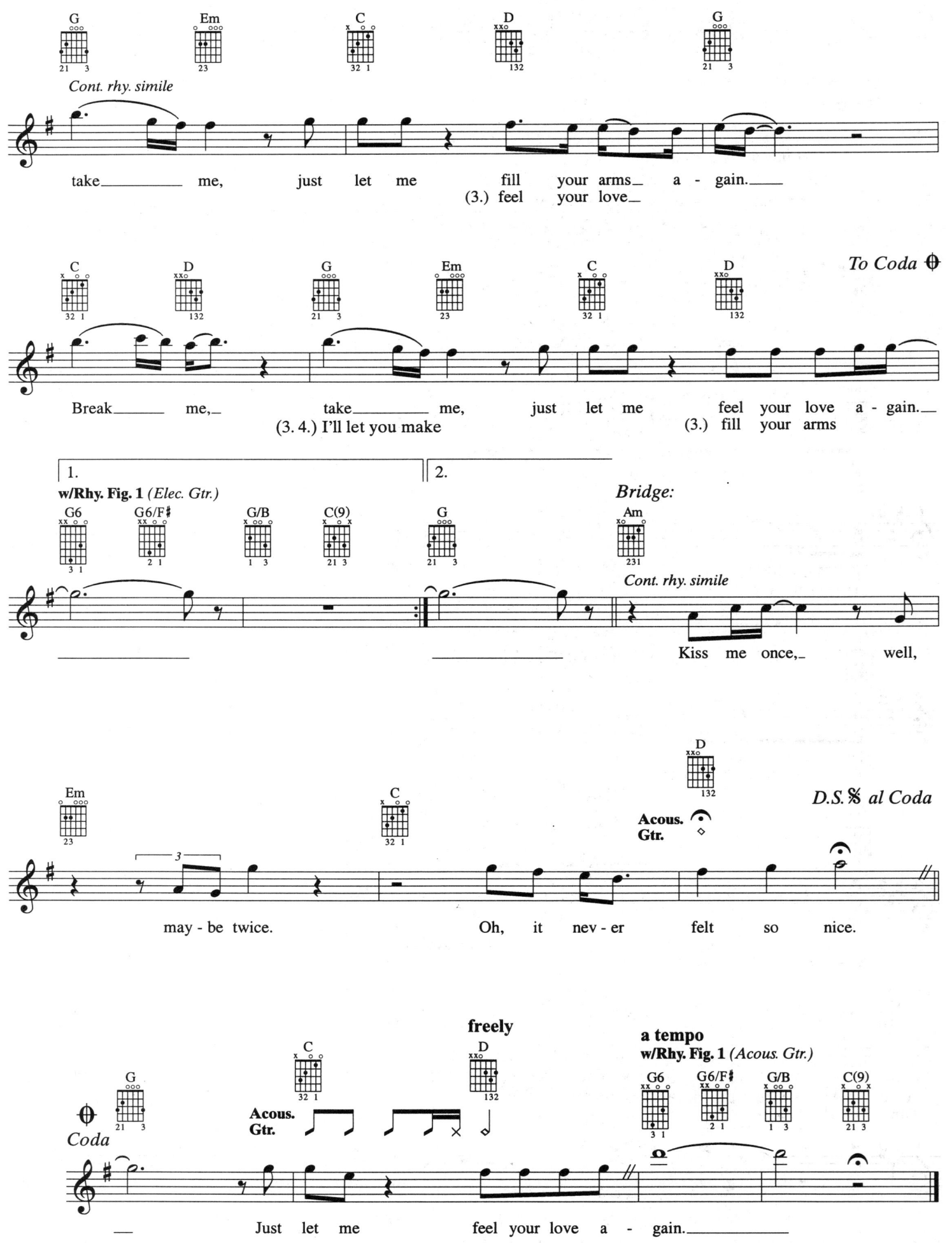

DO YOU WANT TO PLAY?

Acous. Gtr. w/Drop D tuning:
⑥ = D

Words and Music by
JEWEL KILCHER

1. Met her on a Fri - day af - ter - noon,___ in a ne - on day-glo pink chif - fon___ sat - in room.___ She nev - er looks back,___ ___ oh, she al - ways looked good dressed in black.

2. She lived be - neath the dis - co dis - count store,___ with pic - tures of Ran - dy New - man scat - tered all a - cross the floor.___ I said, "This place looks sort of des - o - late." She said, "Are you on - ly half a - live or have you al - ways been this in - ar - tic - u - late?"

Chorus:

Oh,_____ you're so spe - cial. Oh,_____ who gives a...

Do You Want to Play? - 3 - 1
0643B

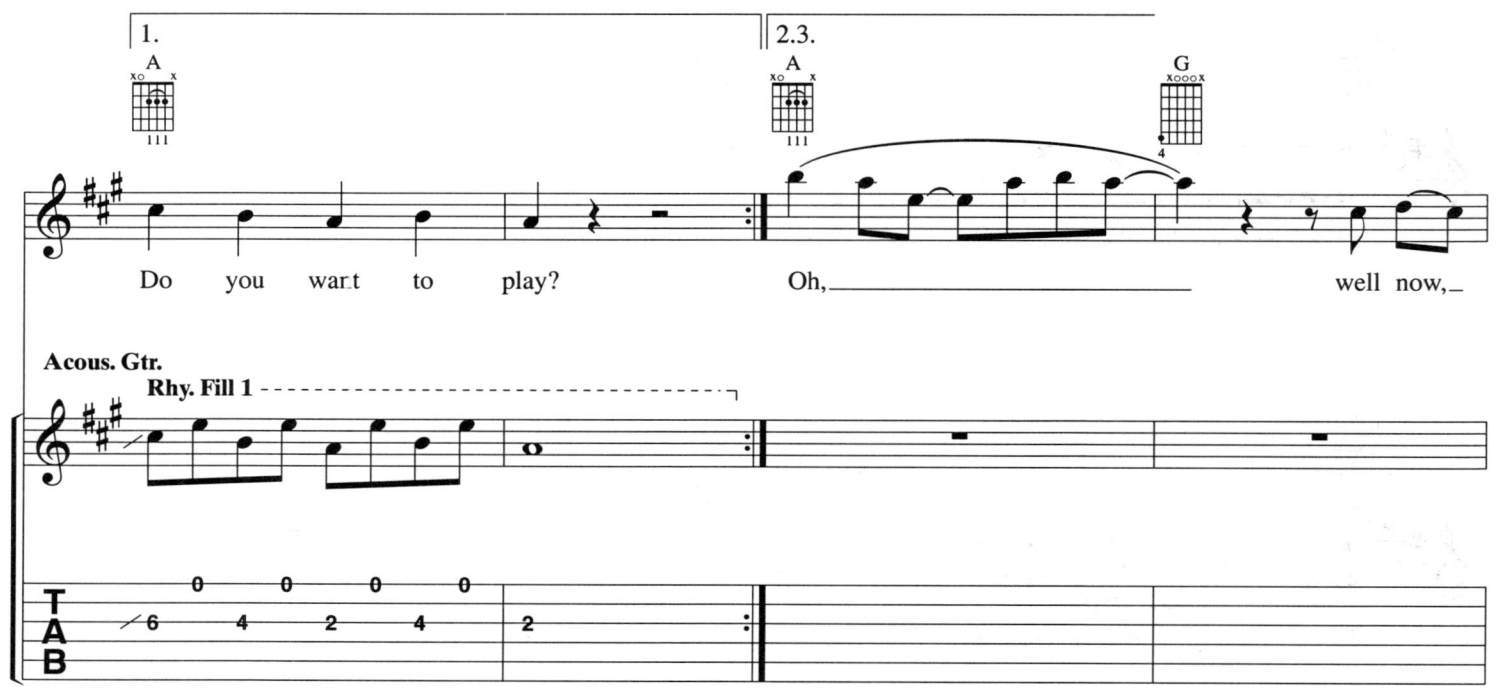

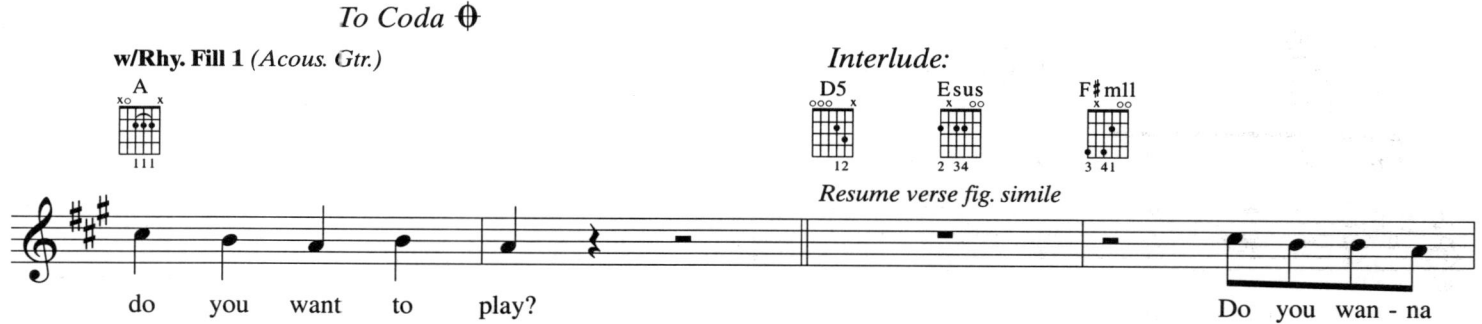

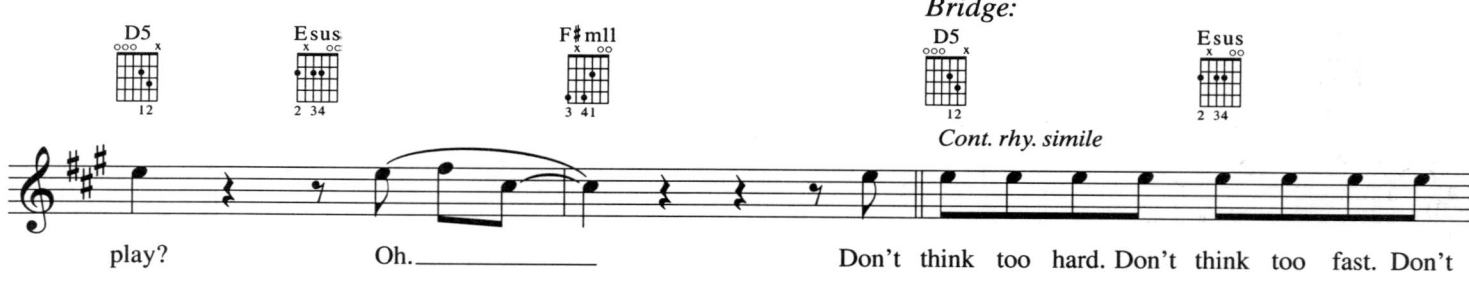

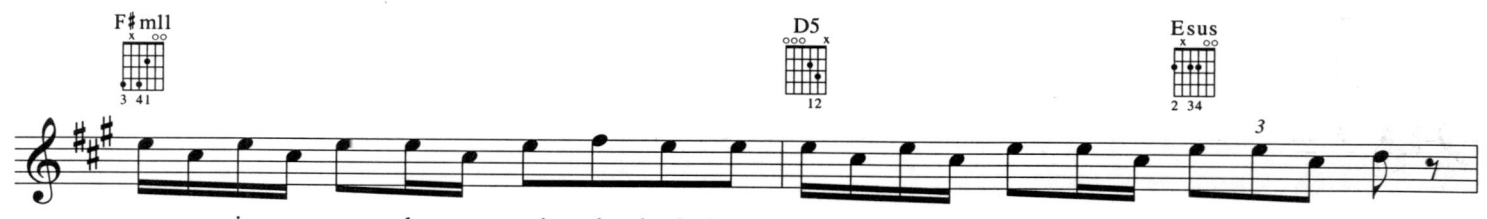

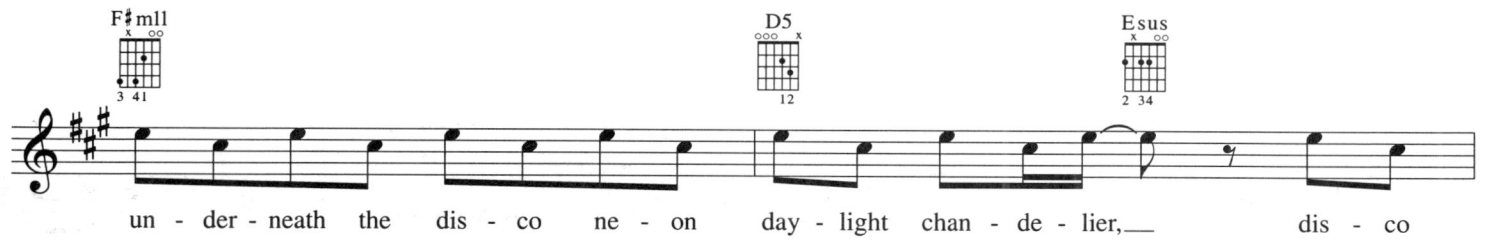

un - der-neath the dis - co ne - on day - light chan - de - lier,___ dis - co

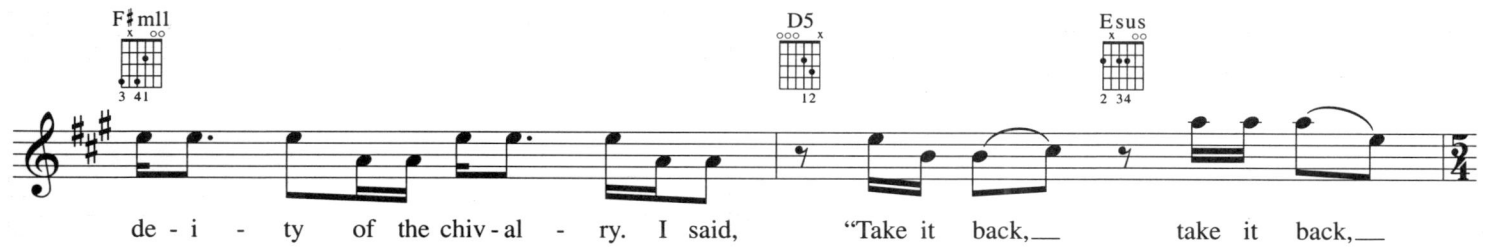

de - i - ty of the chiv - al - ry. I said, "Take it back,___ take it back,___

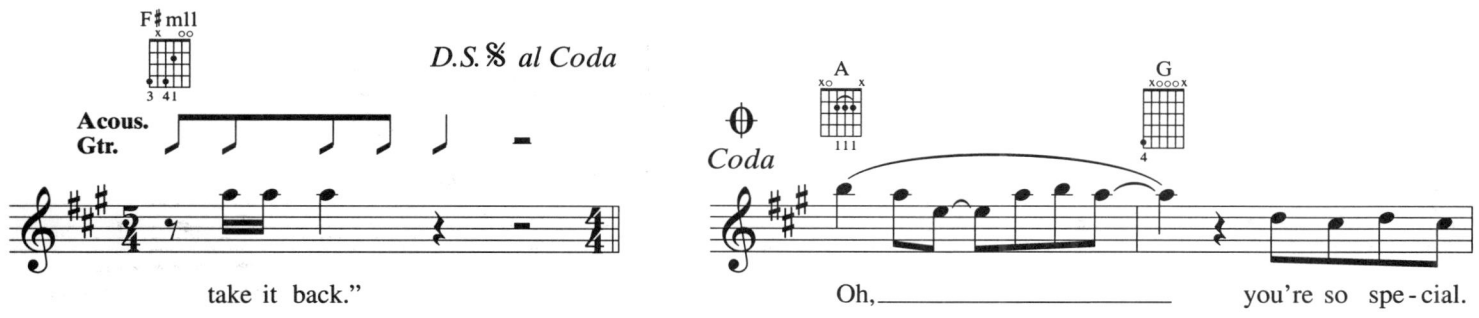

Acous. Gtr.

D.S. ℅ *al Coda*

Coda

take it back."

Oh,___ you're so spe-cial.

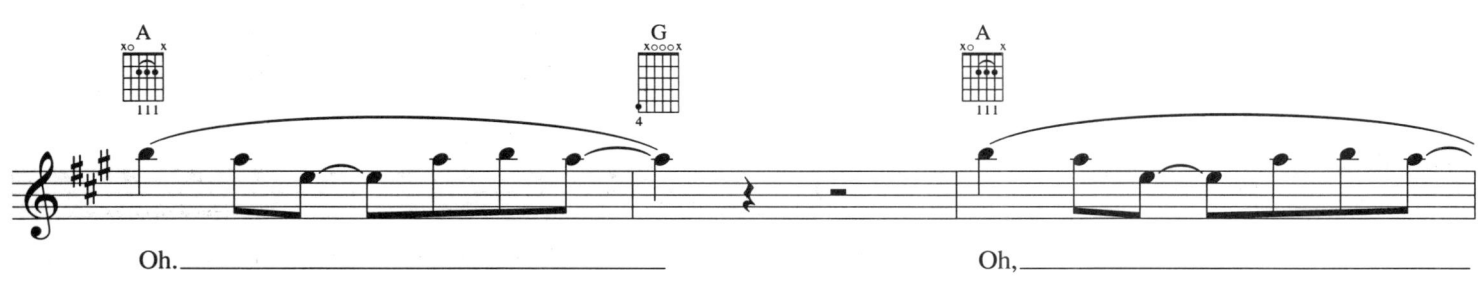

Oh.___ Oh,___

w/Rhy. Fill 1 *(Acous. Gtr.)*

___ who gives a... Do you want to play?

TILL WE RUN OUT OF ROAD

Words and Music by
JEWEL KILCHER and TY MURRAY

All gtrs. w/capo II

Till We Run Out of Road - 5 - 2
0643B

Bridge:

pen - sive cabs and sh**-ty food washed down with__ can-celled flights. Oh, missed

wake up calls,_ missed_ hol - i - days._ You miss your boy and wife._

All the late night drives_ that cause_ the dawn to strike you like a

knife._ Hey,_____ man, this is a beau - ti-ful

life. We're leav - ing_____ a - gain,_

leav-ing a - gain._ Oh, we're leav -

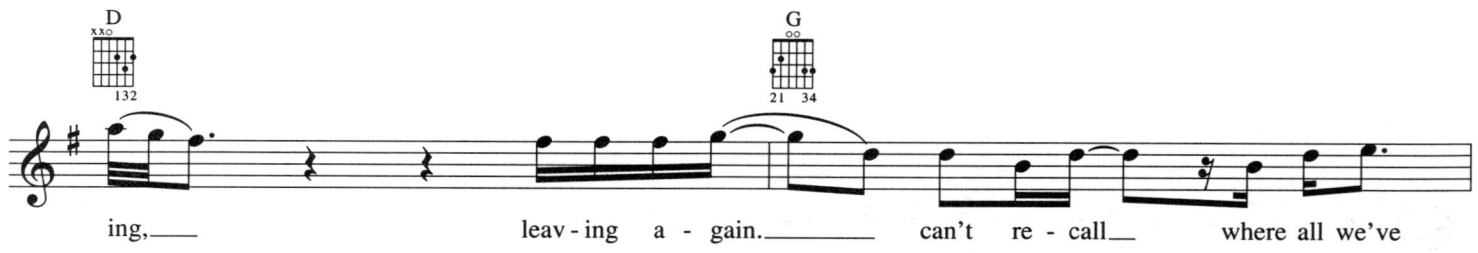

ing,_____ leav-ing a - gain._____ can't re-call___ where all we've

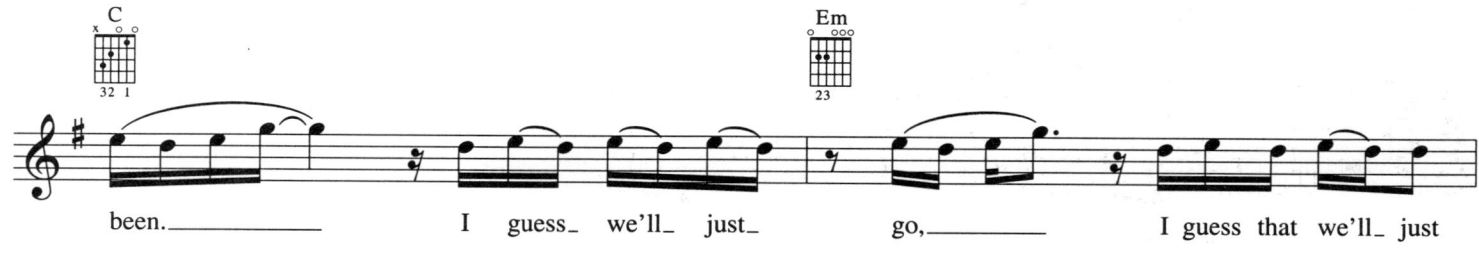

been._____ I guess_ we'll_ just_ go,_____ I guess that we'll_ just

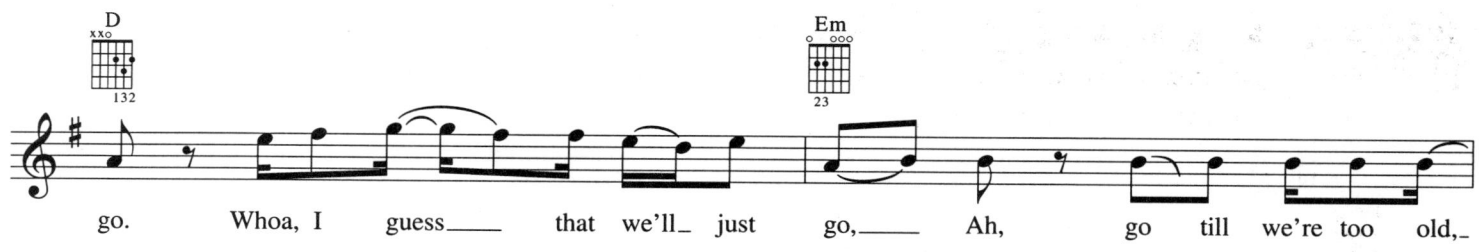

go. Whoa, I guess_____ that we'll_ just go,_____ Ah, go till we're too old,_

_ or we run_ out_ of_ road._____ Oh,_ yeah. Oh,_____ oh._

Outro: w/ad lib. vocal

(2nd time) leav - ing, leav-ing a - gain._ We're

SERVE THE EGO

Words by
JEWEL KILCHER
Music by
JEWEL KILCHER, ITAAL SHUR and CESAR LEMOS

Serve the Ego - 3 - 1
0643B

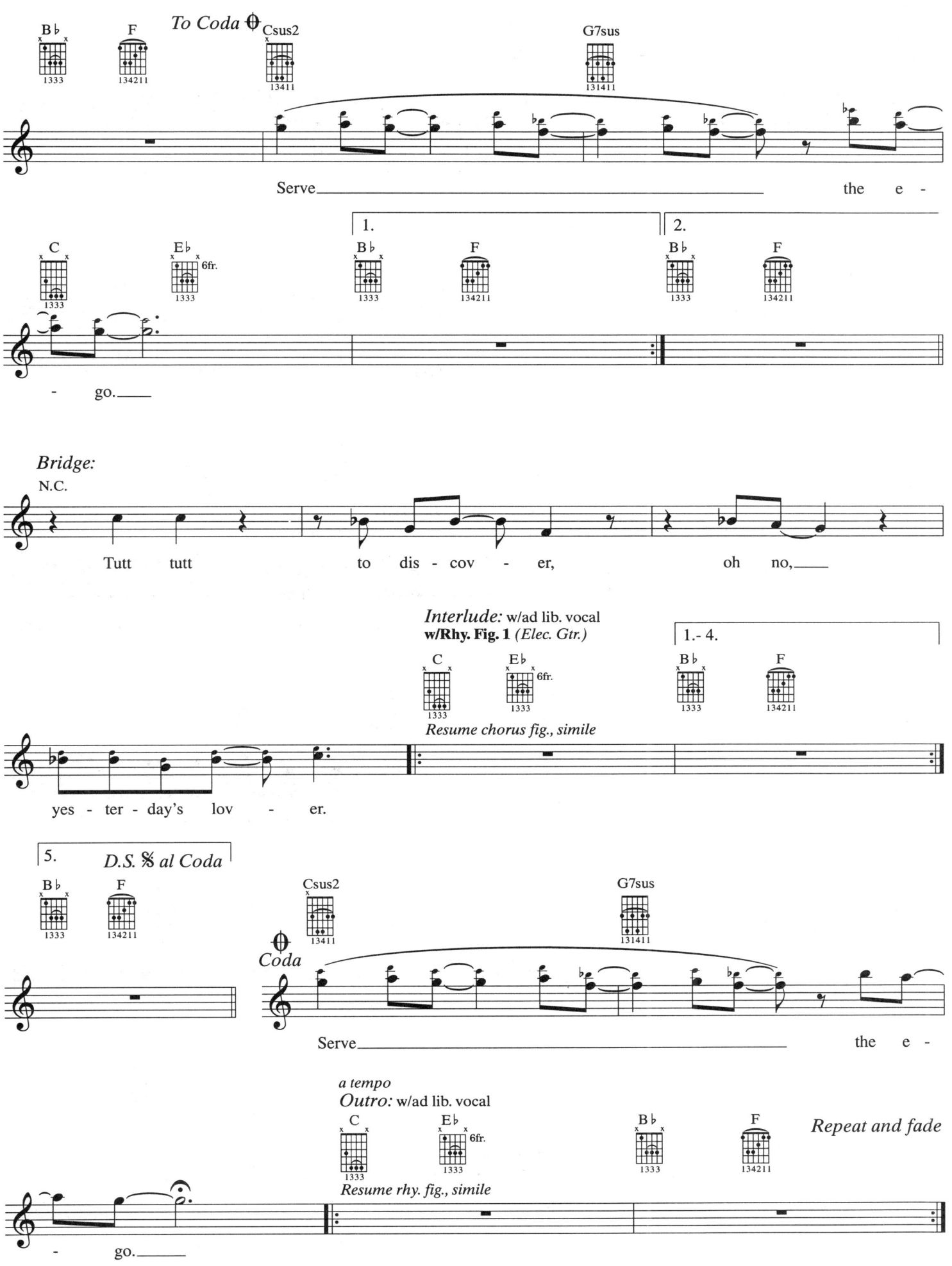

THIS WAY

Words by
JEWEL KILCHER
Music by
JEWEL KILCHER and RICK NOWELS

Acous. Gtr. w/capo IV

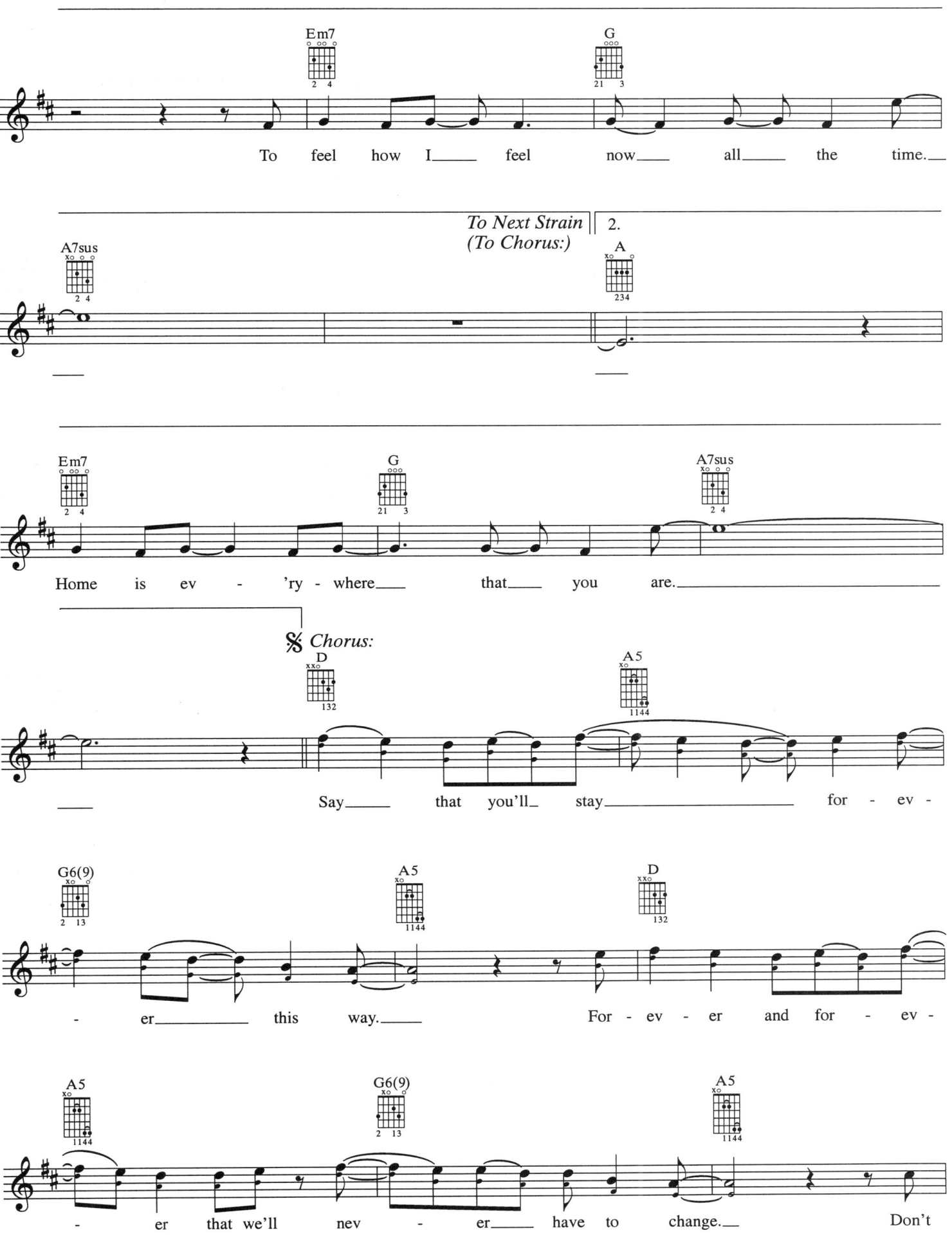

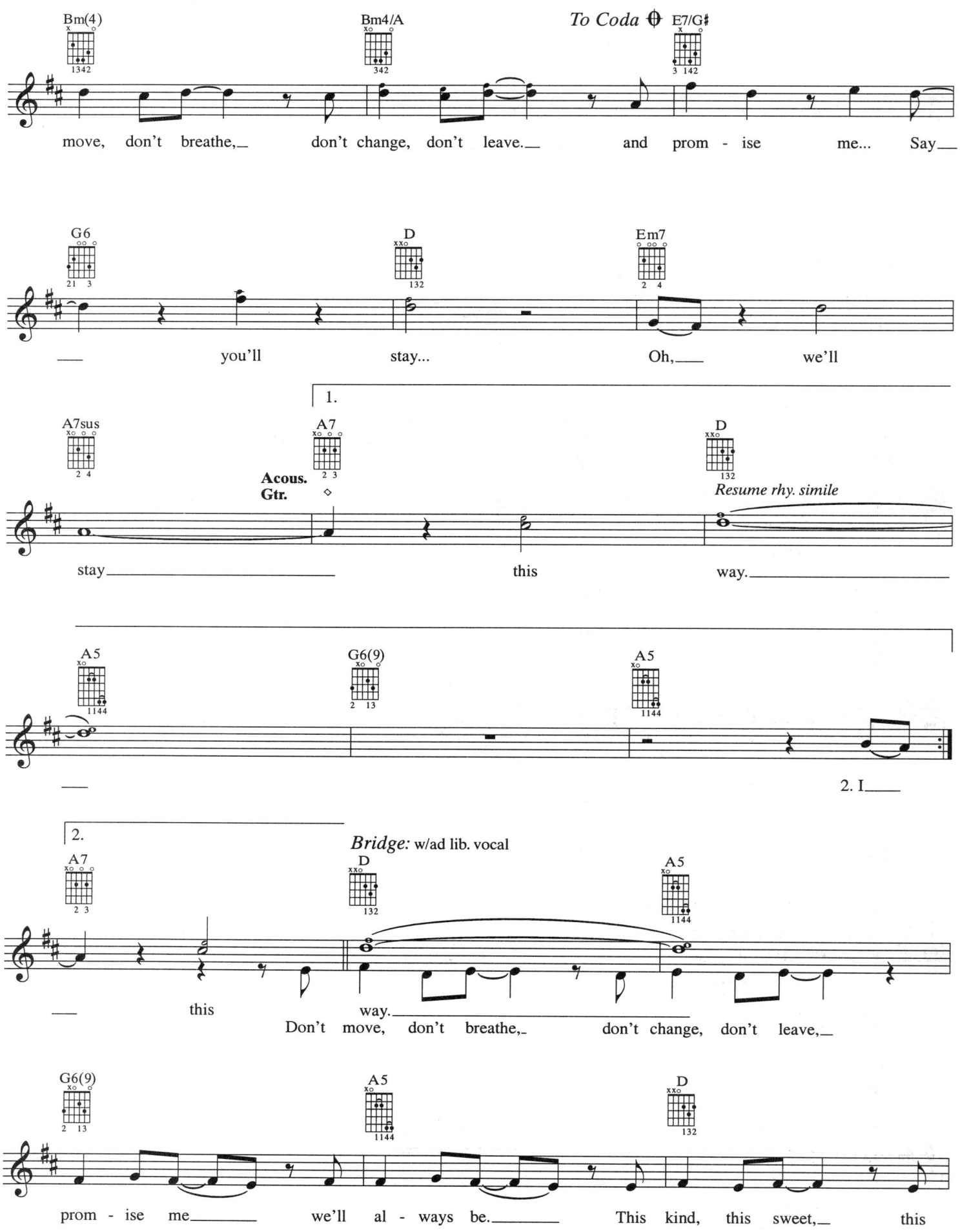

CLEVELAND

Words and Music by
JEWEL KILCHER

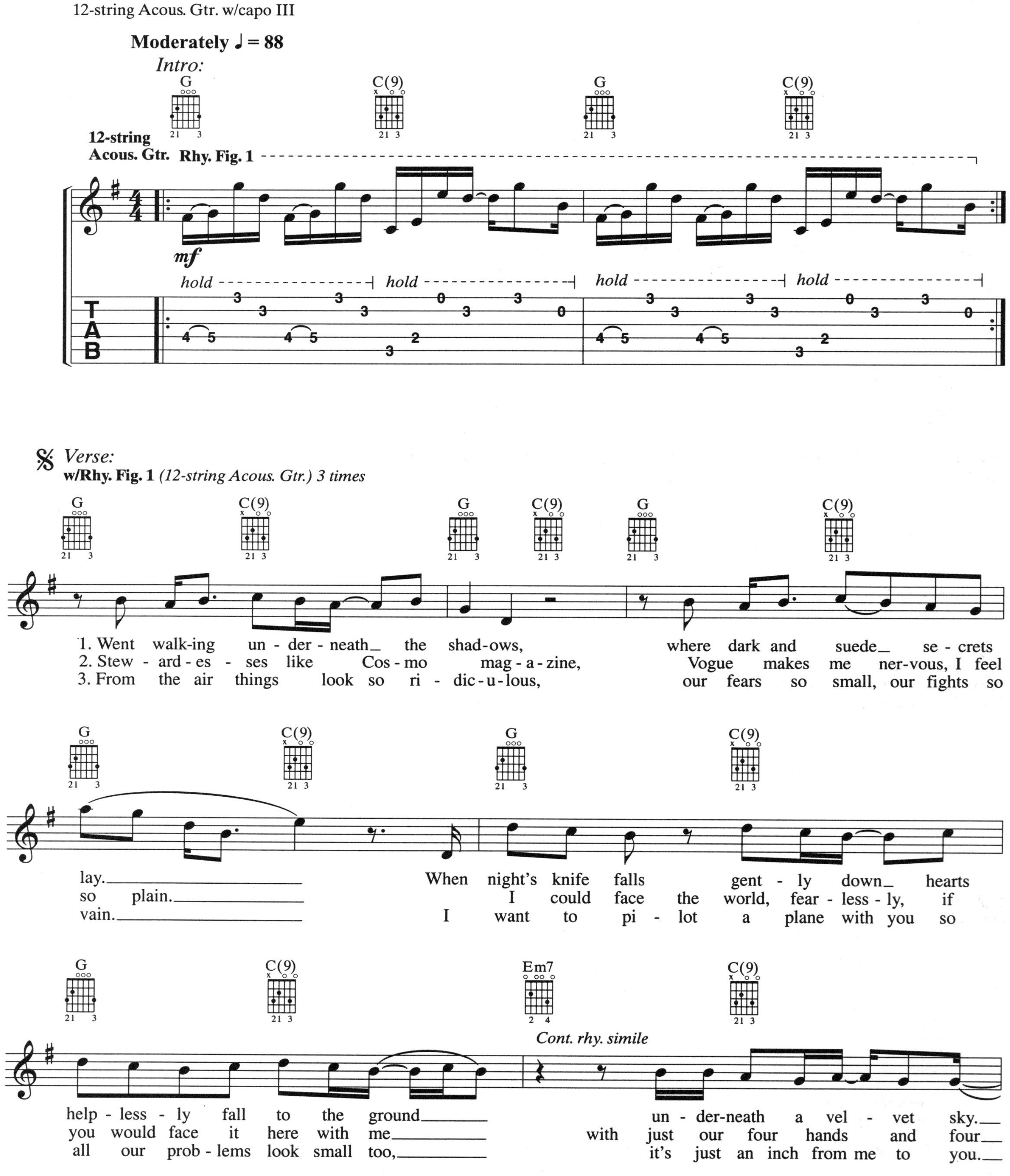

12-string Acous. Gtr. w/capo III

Moderately ♩ = 88

Intro:

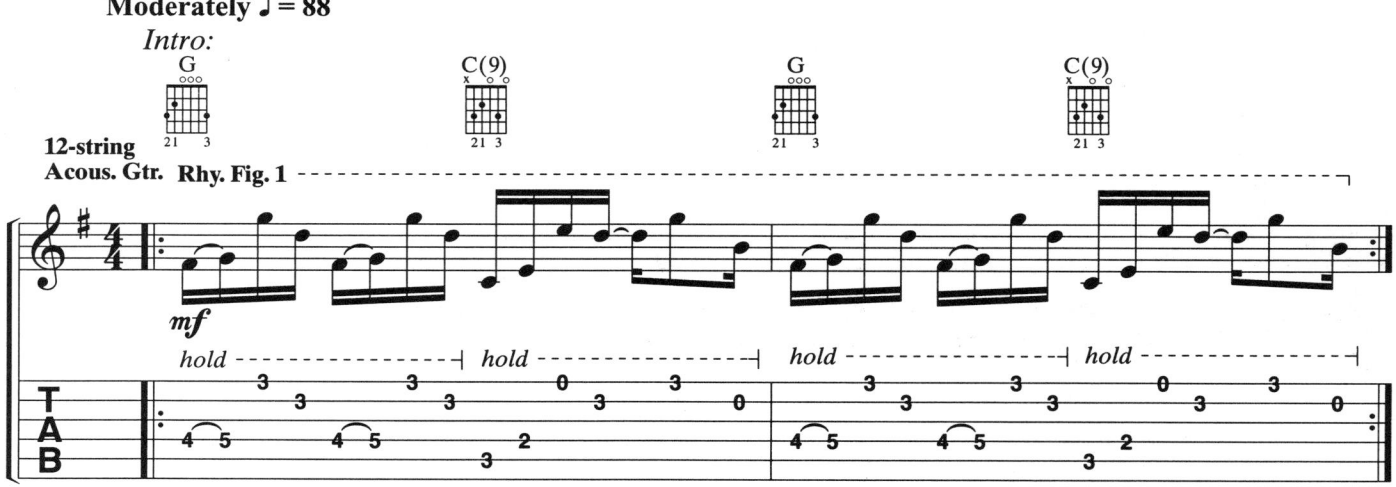

Verse:
w/Rhy. Fig. 1 *(12-string Acous. Gtr.) 3 times*

1. Went walk-ing un-der-neath the shad-ows, where dark and suede se-crets
2. Stew-ard-es-ses like Cos-mo mag-a-zine, Vogue makes me ner-vous, I feel
3. From the air things look so ri-dic-u-lous, our fears so small, our fights so

lay. When night's knife falls gent-ly down hearts
so plain. I could face the world, fear-less-ly, if
vain. I want to pi-lot a plane with you so

Cont. rhy. simile

help-less-ly fall to the ground un-der-neath a vel-vet sky.
you would face it here with me with just our four hands and four
all our prob-lems look small too, it's just an inch from me to you.

Cleveland - 3 - 1
0643B

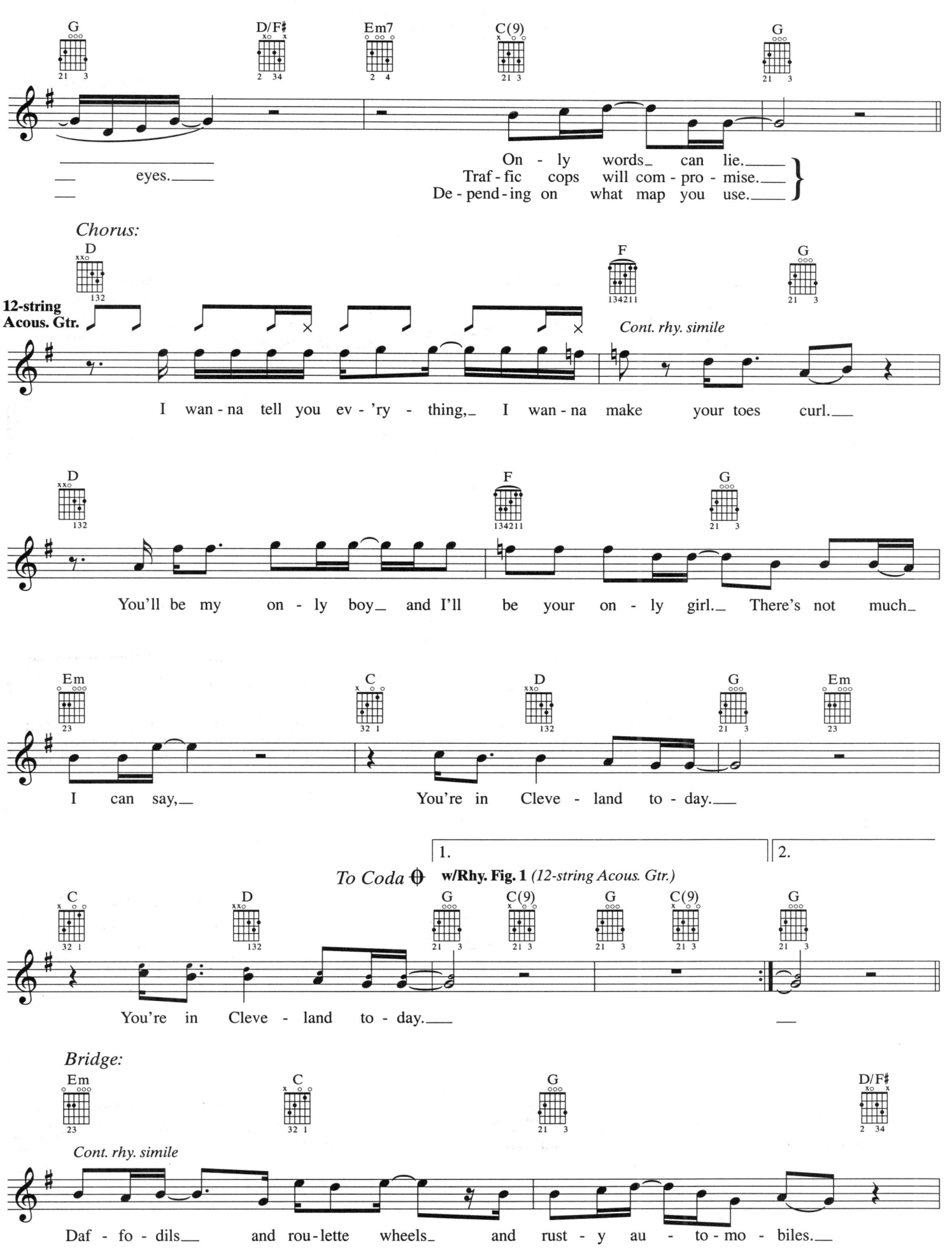

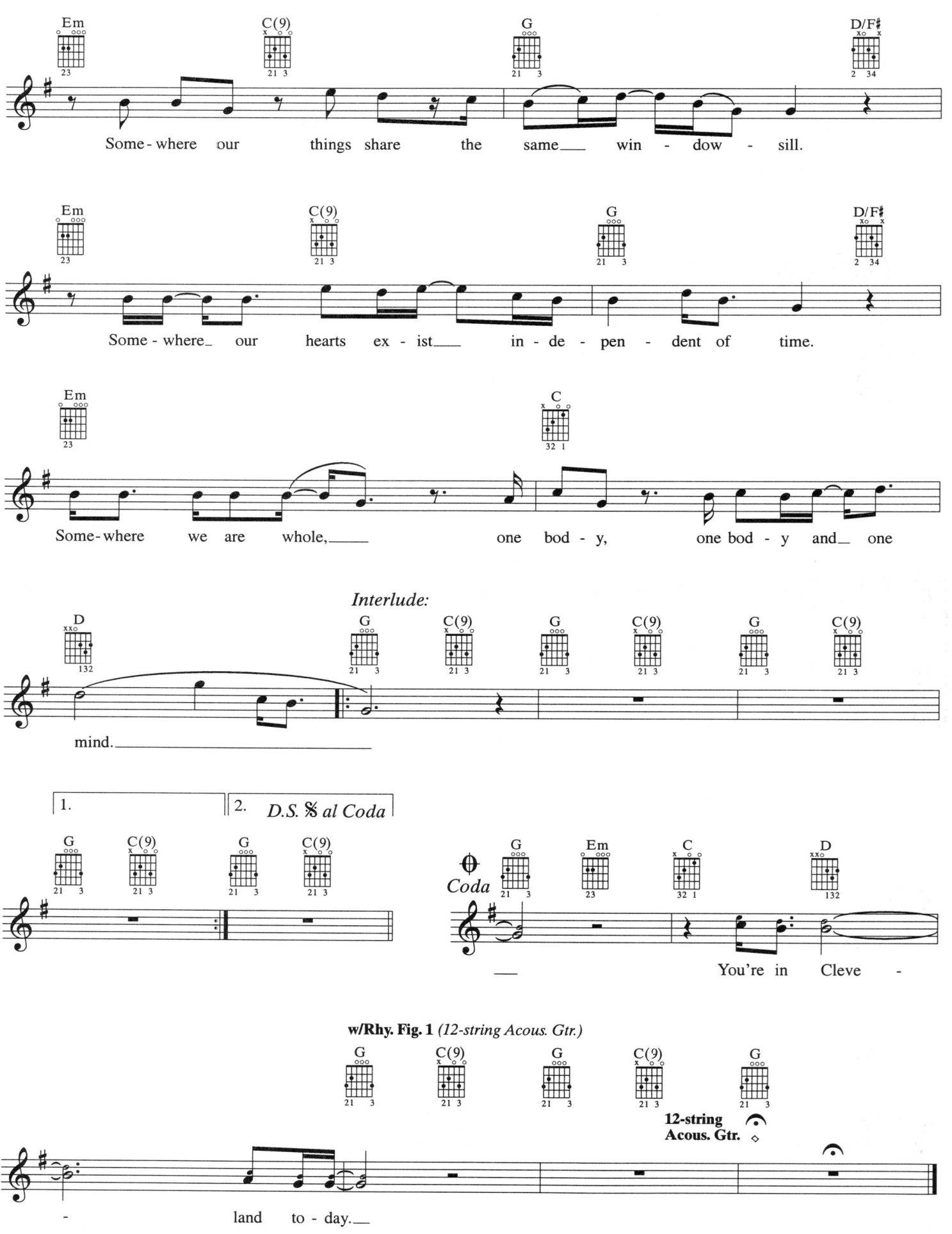

Some-where our things share the same__ win-dow - sill.

Some-where_ our hearts ex - ist__ in - de - pen - dent of time.

Some-where we are whole,_____ one bod - y, one bod - y and_ one

Interlude:

mind._____

1.

2. *D.S. % al Coda*

Coda

_ You're in Cleve -

w/Rhy. Fig. 1 *(12-string Acous. Gtr.)*

12-string
Acous. Gtr.

- land to - day._

I WON'T WALK AWAY

Words by
JEWEL KILCHER
Music by
JEWEL KILCHER and RICK NOWELS

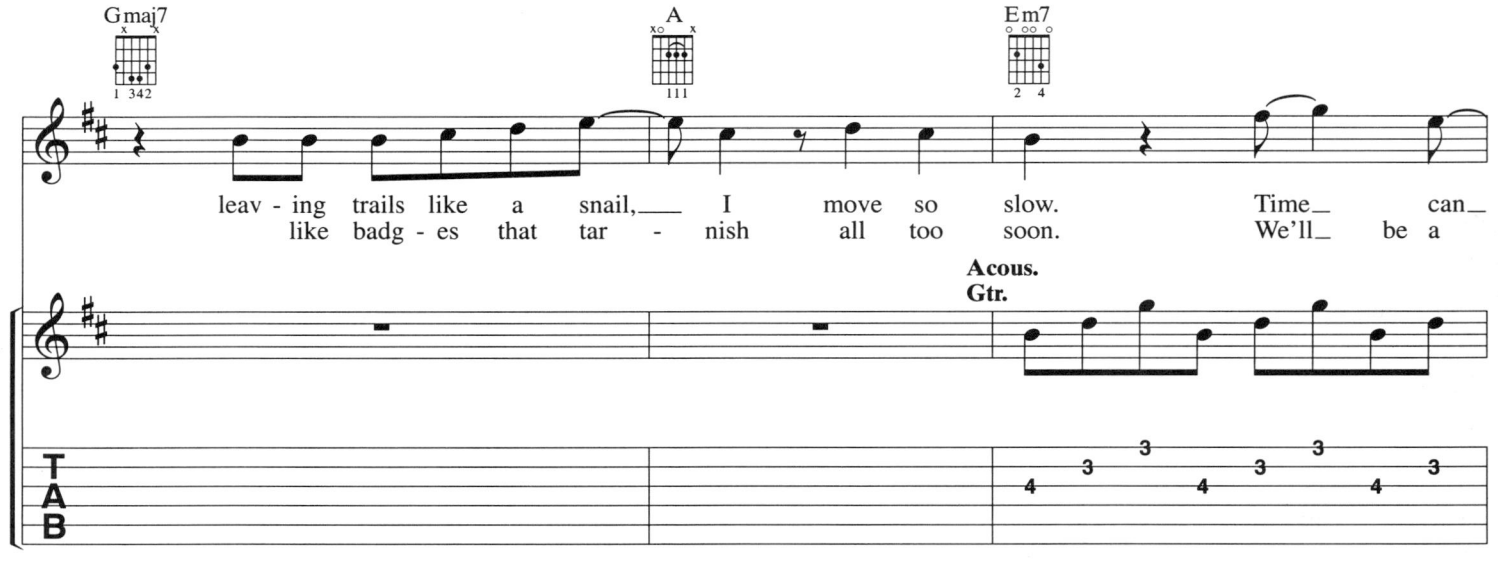

leav - ing trails like a snail,___ I move so slow. Time___ can___
like badg - es that tar - nish all too soon. We'll___ be a

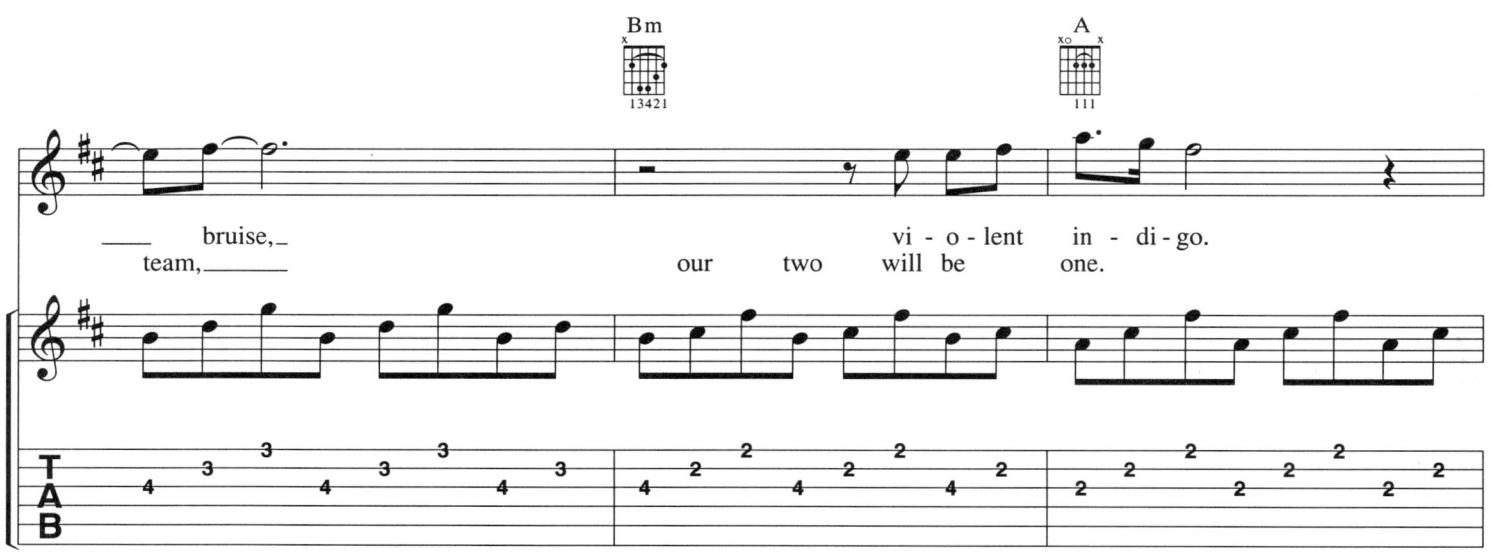

___ bruise,___ vi - o - lent in - di - go.
team,_____ our two will be one.

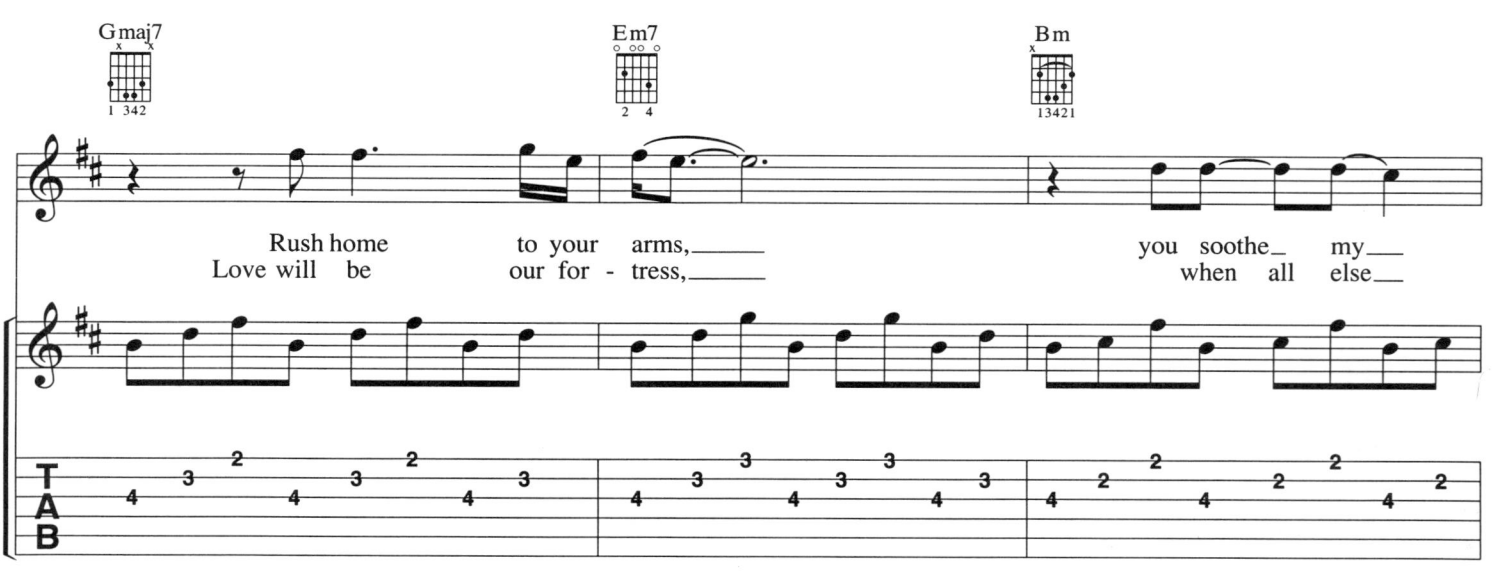

Rush home to your arms,_____ you soothe___ my___
Love will be our for - tress,_____ when all else___

38

LOVE ME, JUST LEAVE ME ALONE

Words and Music by
JEWEL KILCHER

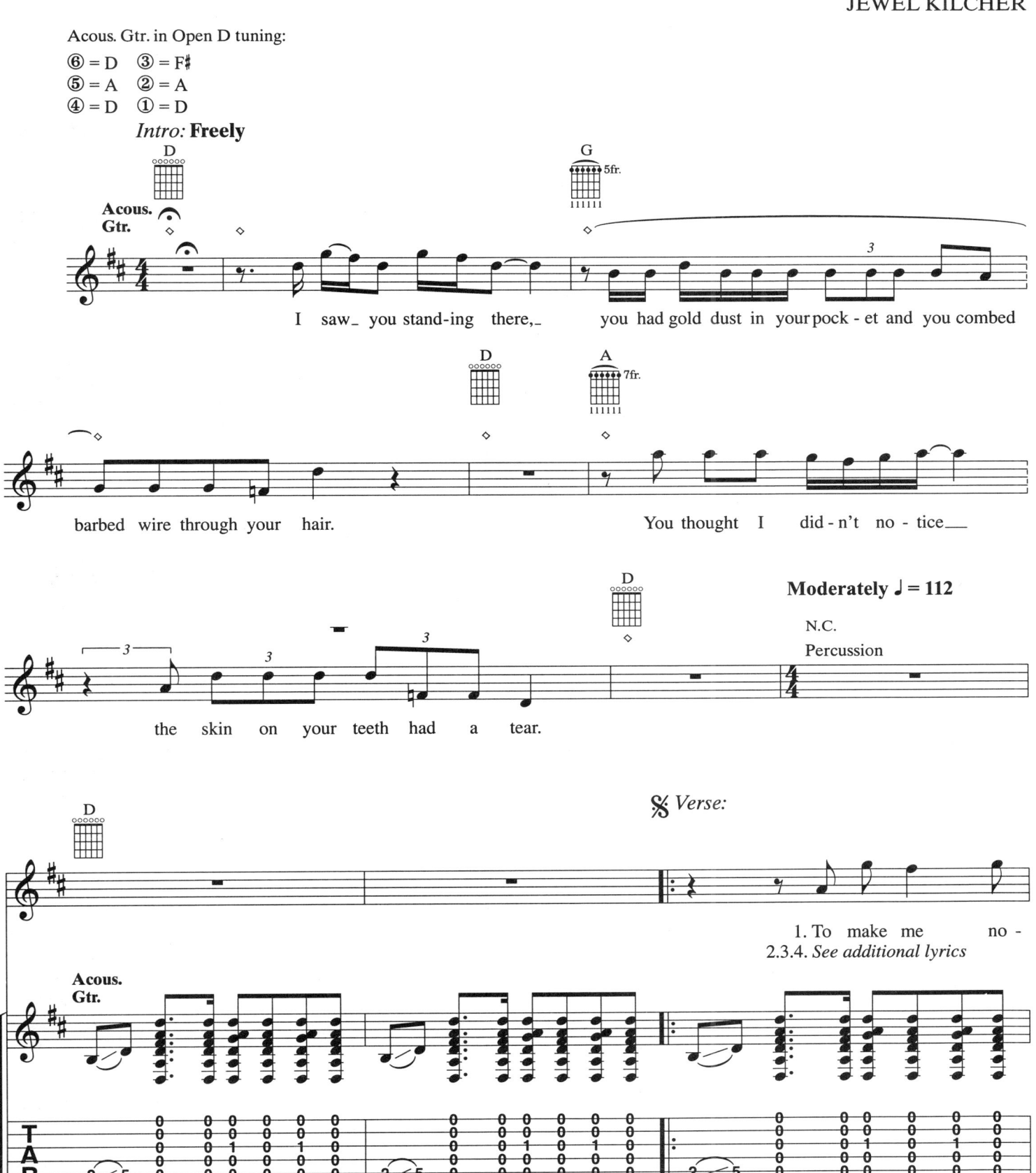

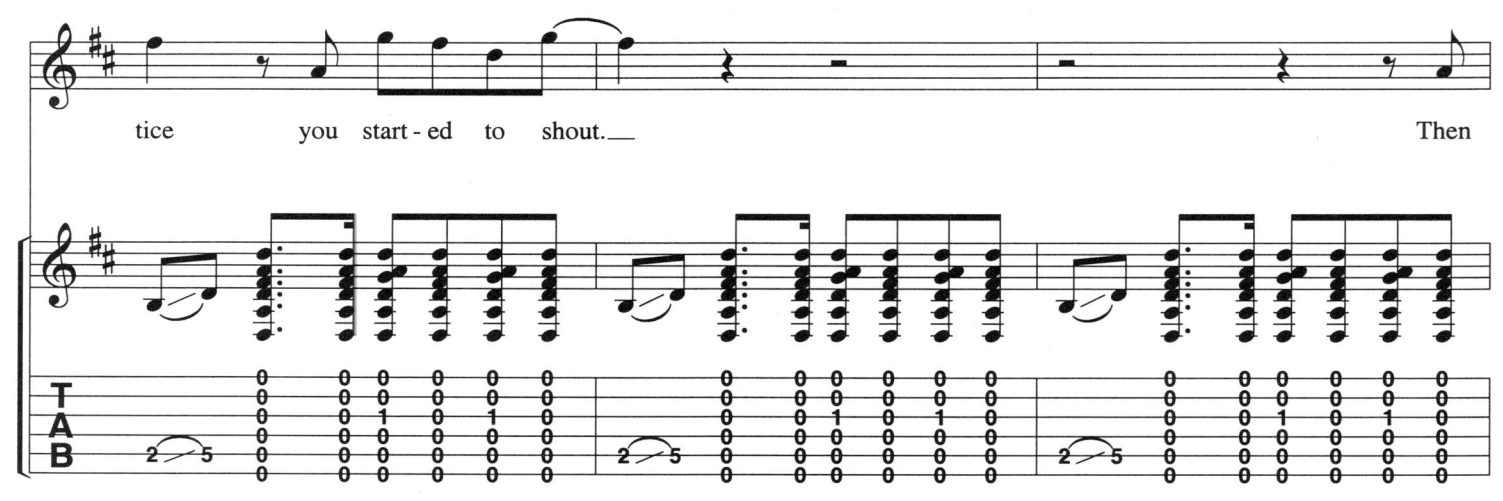

tice   you start - ed to   shout.___   Then

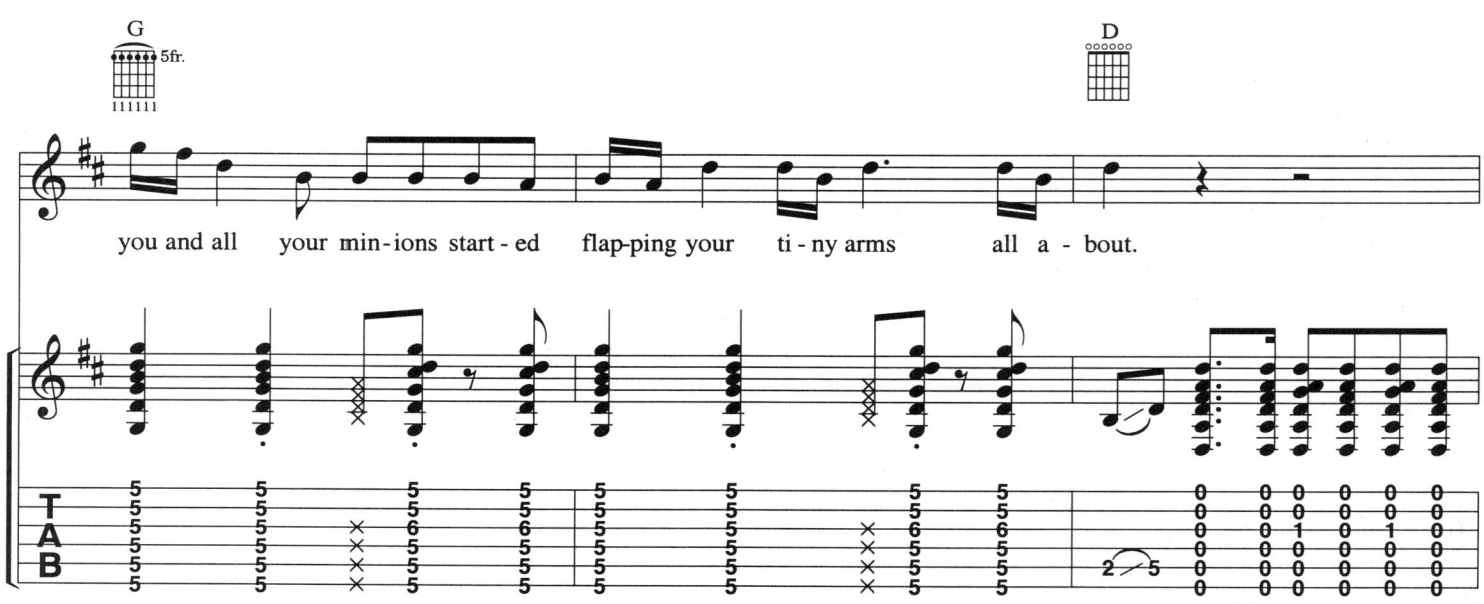

you and all   your min - ions start - ed   flap - ping your   ti - ny arms   all a - bout.

They   said you were a wise___ man,   when did they teach   wise men to   pout?___

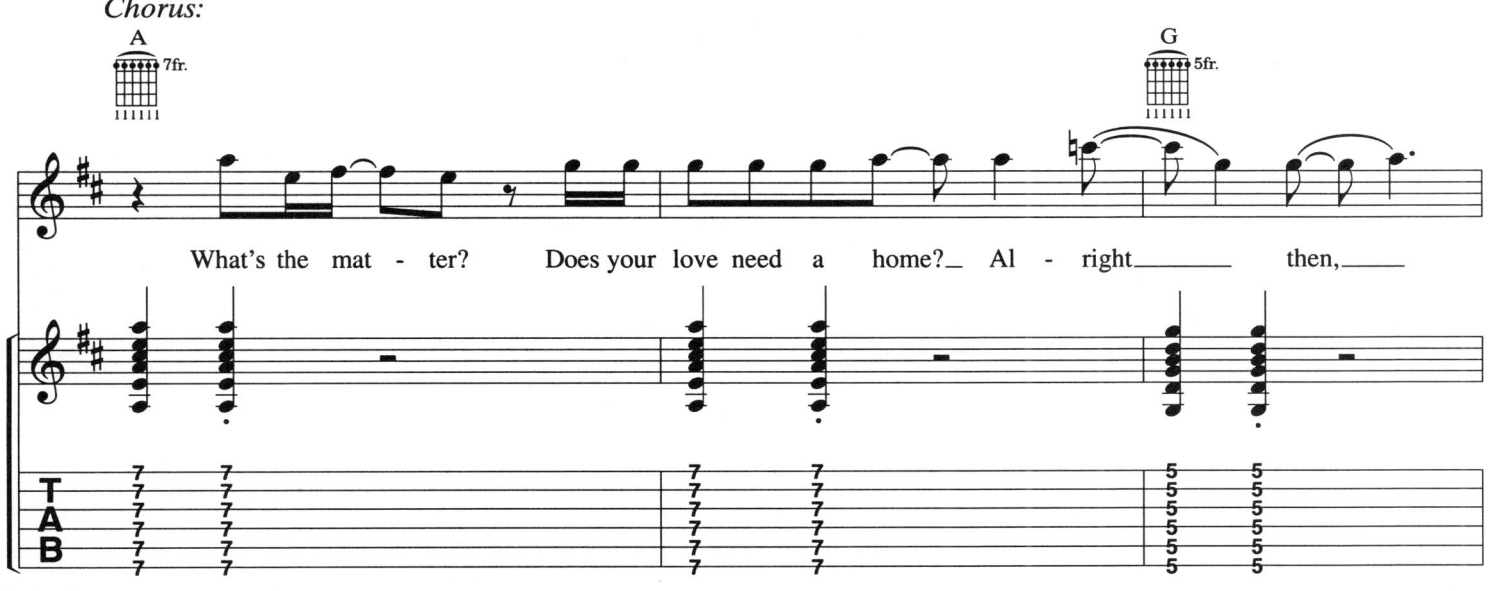

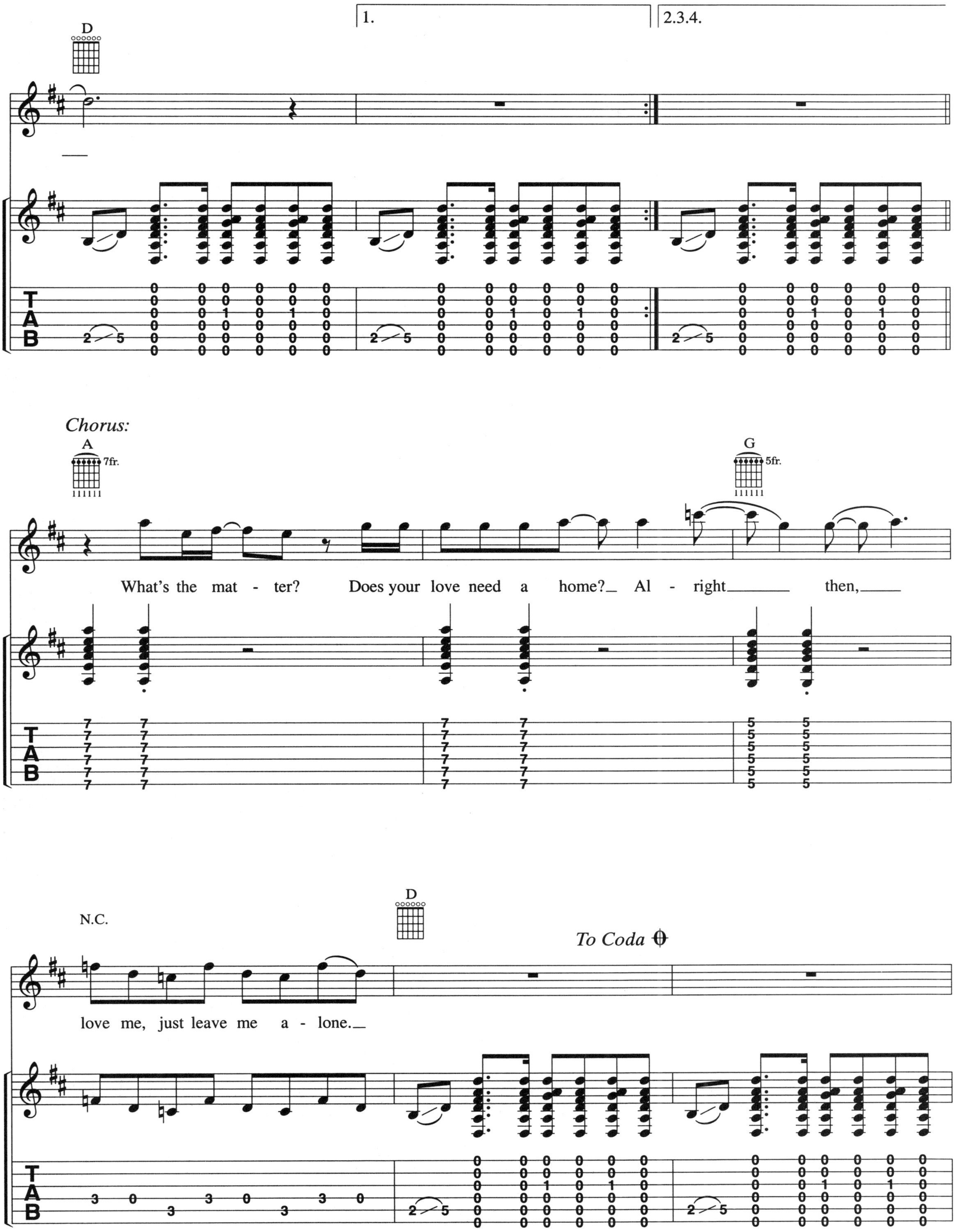

1.
2.3.4.
D
Chorus:
A
7fr.
G
5fr.
What's the mat - ter? Does your love need a home? Al - right then,
N.C.
D
To Coda
love me, just leave me a - lone.
TAB

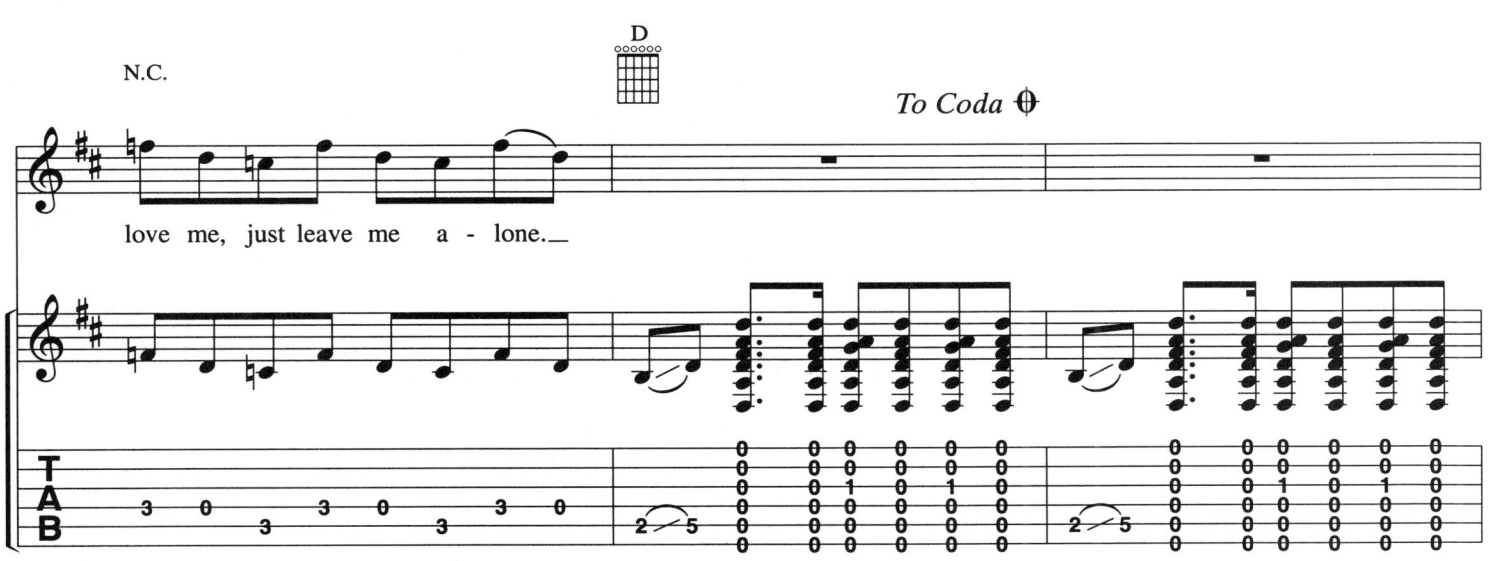

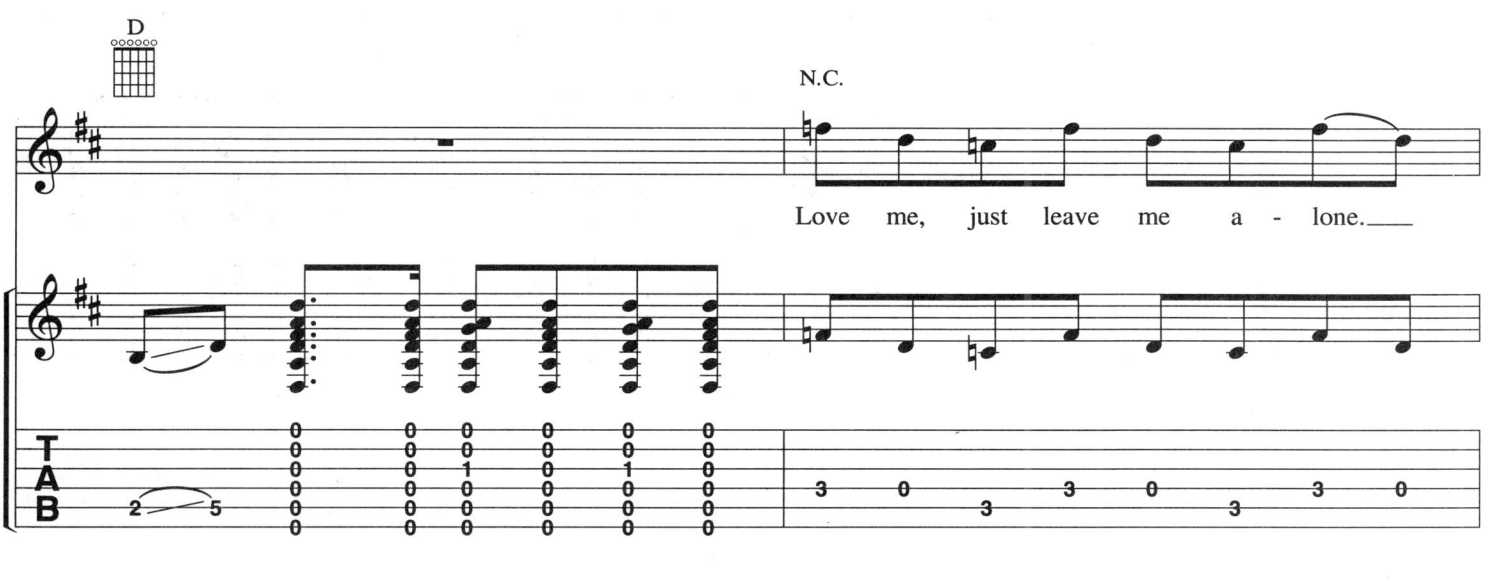

Verse 2:
I tried to forget you but you tied bells to your name.
They jingled every time I thought of you without shame.
I tried to be unlovable, why couldn't you do the same?
(To Chorus:)

Verse 3:
Your mother was a wolf bite, your daddy was a cigarette.
Your brother was a rosebud crossbred with a car wreck.
Your sister was a stockbroker but you ain't nothing but a turtleneck.
(To Chorus:)

Verse 4:
It's not your little boy smile, it's not your little boy name.
It's those big boy hands that are the ones to blame.
I tried to be unlovable, why couldn't you do the same?
(To Chorus:)

THE NEW WILD WEST

Words and Music by
JEWEL KILCHER

Acous. Gtr. w/Drop D tuning:
⑥ = D

Moderately fast waltz ♩ = 160

Intro:

Acous. Gtr. w/Drop D tuning: ⑥ = D.

ghost of the buf - fa - lo mov - ing both fierce and slow. Like

glit - ter - ing pro - phe - cies on the edge of the ho -

ri - zon. As you drive

You see the

Verse 1:

Cont. rhy. simile

The New Wild West - 6 - 1
0643B

Verse 2:

glit - ter - ing high - ways and beat - en up by - ways that

strad - dle and gir - dle our great and man - y faced

na - tion. You see the

Verse 3:

lambs in the ghet - tos who wor - ship their Ge - pet - tos. Be -

liev - ing in, nev - er see - ing the strings they think

bind_____ them. So we

Verse 4:

write to our con - gress - men with bleed - ing pens of the

sor - row with - in._____ And in re - turn they just send

The New Wild West - 6 - 2
0643B

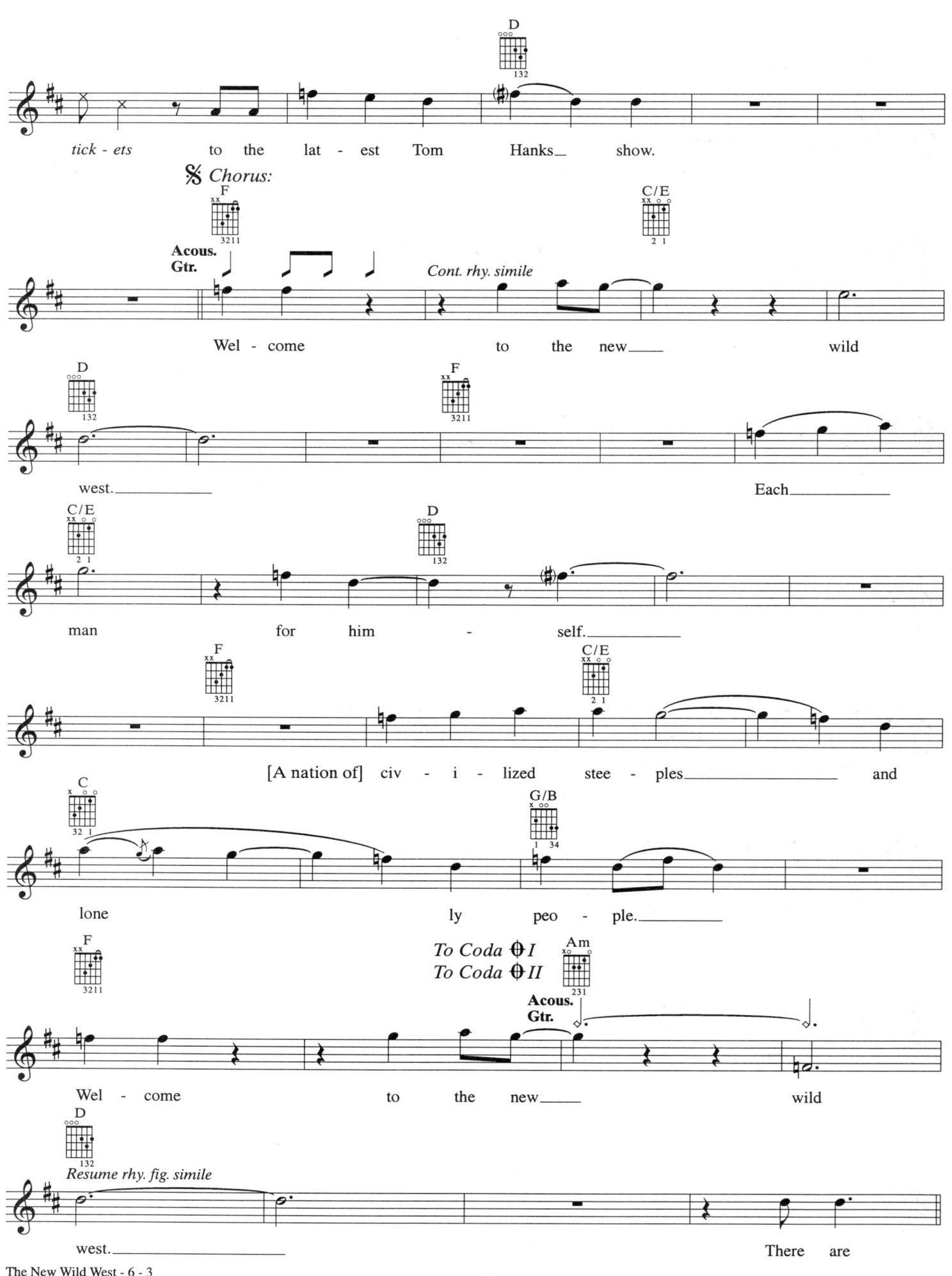

tick - ets to the lat - est Tom Hanks__ show.

§ Chorus:

Wel - come to the new____ wild

west.____

Each____

man for him - self.____

[A nation of] civ - i - lized stee - ples_____ and

lone ly peo - ple.____

Wel - come to the new____ wild

west.____

There are

GREY MATTER

Words and Music by
JEWEL KILCHER

mune to all rea-son, and I'm flat - tered___ by your_ grey

mat-ter._____ mat-ter. And I do not un-der-stand why a

wom-an can't_ just love_ a man._____

___ and I'm bat - tered___

by your___ grey mat - ter._____

Verse 2:
You're a child, but you're malicious,
You're sweet but don't remember my name.
Heads I win and tails I'm lost,
Love equals pain.
(To Chorus:)

Verse 3:
Inside my skin, I feel your tongue,
It's telling me I'm dirty and licking my bones.
A scrape against silence, a knife against a plate,
Makes the sound of need on hate.
(To Chorus:)

Verse 4:
You're amusing, you're a real cool show,
With your meat hooks and barbed wire carnival.
You've got gold dust in your pocket,
You've got moth holes in your soul,
From too many false teeth and greasy flashbulbs.
(To Chorus:)

SOMETIMES IT BE THAT WAY

Acous. Gtr. w/capo II

Words and Music by
JEWEL KILCHER

Bright waltz ♩ = 176

Intro:

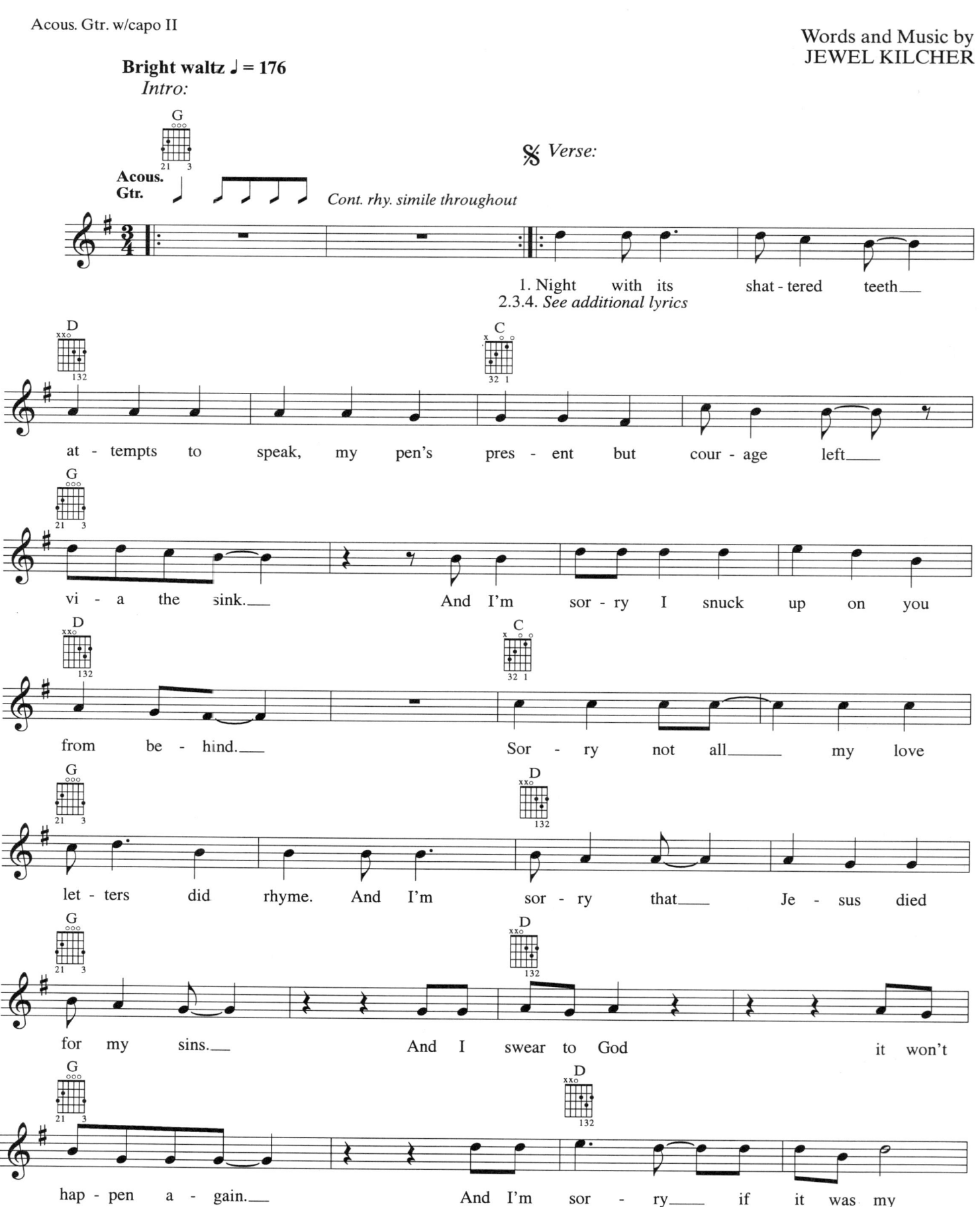

1. Night with its shat-tered teeth
2.3.4. *See additional lyrics*

at-tempts to speak, my pen's pres-ent but cour-age left

vi-a the sink. And I'm sor-ry I snuck up on you

from be-hind. Sor-ry not all my love

let-ters did rhyme. And I'm sor-ry that Je-sus died

for my sins. And I swear to God it won't

hap-pen a-gain. And I'm sor-ry if it was my

Sometimes It Be That Way - 3 - 1
0643B

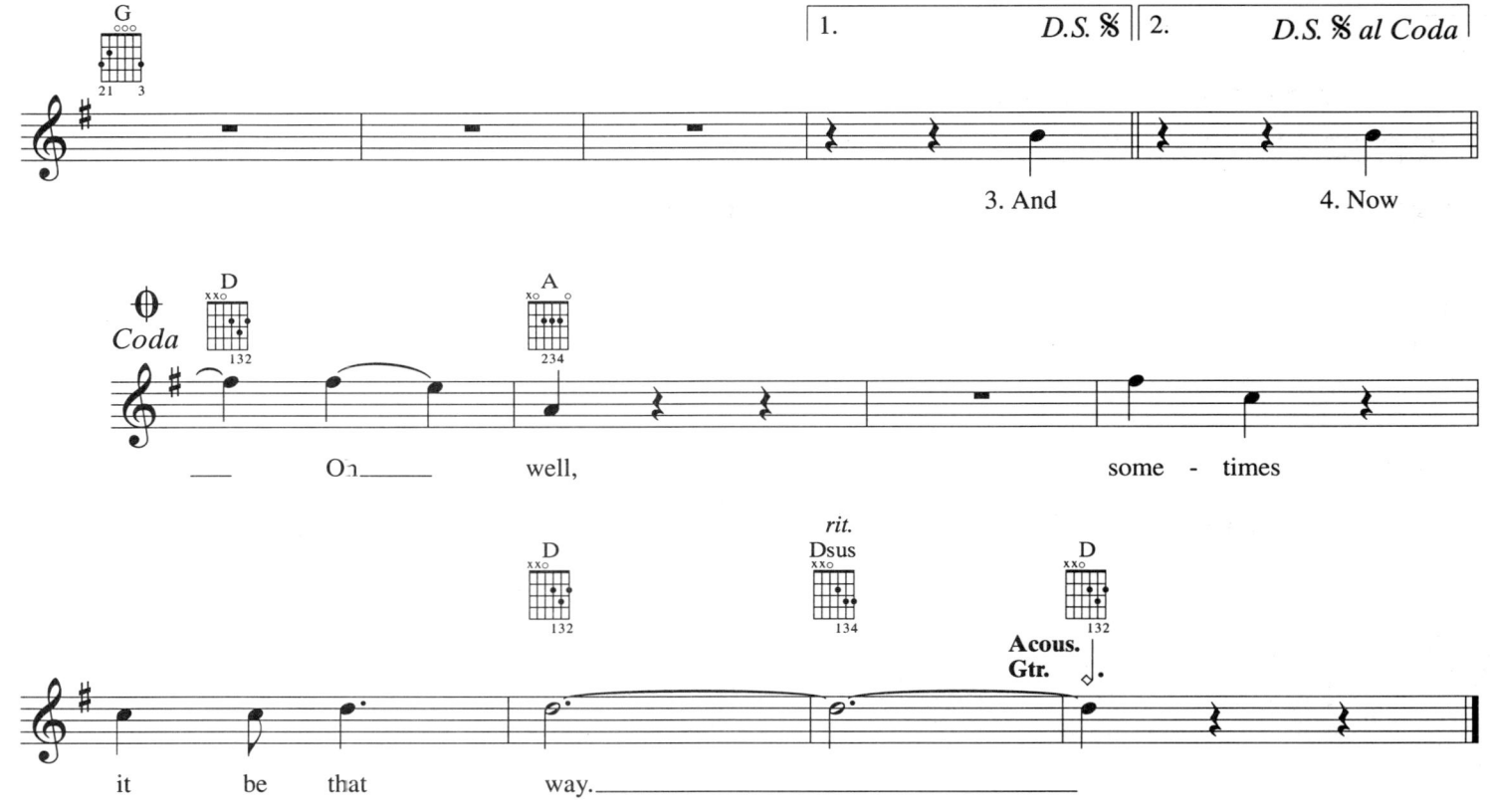

Verse 2:
And Romeo, he was a very nice man.
He said, "Jewel, I don't think you quite understand."
And I'm sorry if you had to explain it like this,
Sorry I was a point you were destined to miss.
And I'm sorry I spoke to you irreverently,
Down in the hollow by the old olive tree.
And I'm sorry if my heart breaking ruined your day.
Oh well, sometimes it be that way.

Verse 3:
And Aphrodite with her neon lamp,
Kissed Neptune, they put her face on a stamp.
And I'm sorry I used it to mail a letter to you,
Sorry, I'm glue and the rest bounces off of you.
And I'm sorry not even this jet's metal wings,
Could get across these simple things.
And I'm sorry if I ever sang your name in vain.
Oh well, sometimes it be that way.
(To Chorus:)

Verse 4:
Now flame licks the air with its silver tongue,
Night has many hands but I have just one.
And I'm sorry I walked in on you unexpectedly,
Sorry I didn't serve you both chamomile tea.
And I'm sorry I didn't always have a match
That could start a fire big enough for your heart to catch.
And I'm sorry if it was my heart breaking that ruined your day,
Oh well, sometimes it be that way.
(To Chorus:)

GUITAR TAB GLOSSARY **

TABLATURE EXPLANATION

READING TABLATURE: Tablature illustrates the six strings of the guitar. Notes and chords are indicated by the placement of fret numbers on a given string(s).

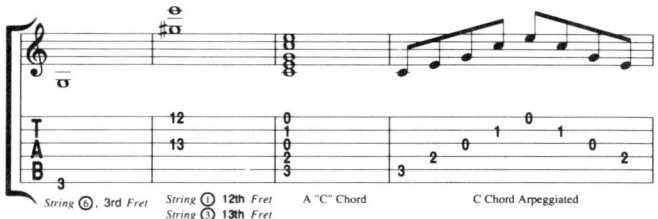

String ⑥, 3rd Fret   String ① 12th Fret   A "C" Chord   C Chord Arpeggiated
                      String ③ 13th Fret

BENDING NOTES

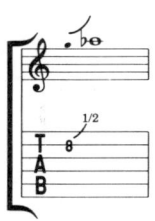

HALF STEP: Play the note and bend string one half step.*

PREBEND (Ghost Bend): Bend to the specified note, before the string is picked.

WHOLE STEP: Play the note and bend string one whole step.

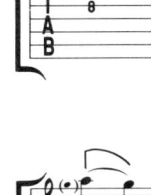

PREBEND AND RELEASE: Bend the string, play it, then release to the original note.

WHOLE STEP AND A HALF: Play the note and bend string a whole step and a half.

REVERSE BEND: Play the already-bent string, then immediately drop it down to the fretted note.

SLIGHT BEND (Microtone): Play the note and bend string slightly to the equivalent of half a fret.

BEND AND RELEASE: Play the note and gradually bend to the next pitch, then release to the original note. Only the first note is attacked.

*A half step is the smallest interval in Western music; it is equal to one fret. A whole step equals two frets.

UNISON BEND: Play both notes and immediately bend the lower note to the same pitch as the higher note.

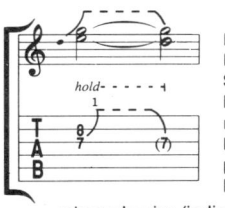

DOUBLE NOTE BEND: Play both notes and immediately bend both strings simultaneously.

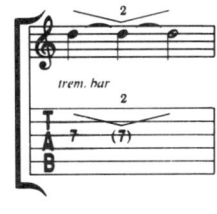

BENDS INVOLVING MORE THAN ONE STRING: Play the note and bend string while playing an additional note (or notes) on another string(s). Upon release, relieve pressure from additional note(s), causing original note to sound alone.

BENDS INVOLVING STATIONARY NOTES: Play notes and bend lower pitch, then hold until release begins (indicated at the point where line becomes solid).

TREMOLO BAR

SPECIFIED INTERVAL: The pitch of a note or chord is lowered to a specified interval and then may or may not return to the original pitch. The activity of the tremolo bar is graphically represented by peaks and valleys.

UN-SPECIFIED INTERVAL: The pitch of a note or a chord is lowered to an unspecified interval.

HARMONICS

NATURAL HARMONIC: A finger of the fret hand lightly touches the note or notes indicated in the tab and is played by the pick hand.

ARTIFICIAL HARMONIC: The first tab number is fretted, then the pick hand produces the harmonic by using a finger to lightly touch the same string at the second tab number (in parenthesis) and is then picked by another finger.

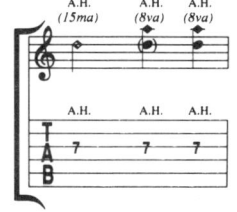

ARTIFICIAL "PINCH" HAR-MONIC: A note is fretted as indicated by the tab, then the pick hand produces the harmonic by squeezing the pick firmly while using the tip of the index finger in the pick attack. If parenthesis are found around the fretted note, it does not sound. No parenthesis means both the fretted note and A.H. are heard simultaneously.

**By Kenn Chipkin and Aaron Stang

RHYTHM SLASHES

STRUM INDICATIONS: Strum with indicated rhythm. The chord voicings are found on the first page of the transcription underneath the song title.

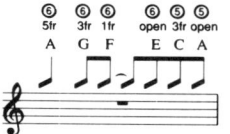

INDICATING SINGLE NOTES USING RHYTHM SLASHES: Very often single notes are incorporated into a rhythm part. The note name is indicated above the rhythm slash with a fret number and a string indication.

ARTICULATIONS

HAMMER ON: Play lower note, then "hammer on" to higher note with another finger. Only the first note is attacked.

LEFT HAND HAMMER: Hammer on the first note played on each string with the left hand.

PULL OFF: Play higher note, then "pull off" to lower note with another finger. Only the first note is attacked.

FRETBOARD TAPPING: "Tap" onto the note indicated by + with a finger of the pick hand, then pull off to the following note held by the fret hand.

TAP SLIDE: Same as fretboard tapping, but the tapped note is slid randomly up the fretboard, then pulled off to the following note.

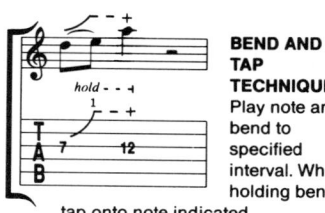

BEND AND TAP TECHNIQUE: Play note and bend to specified interval. While holding bend, tap onto note indicated.

LEGATO SLIDE: Play note and slide to the following note. (Only first note is attacked).

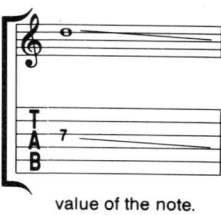

LONG GLISSANDO: Play note and slide in specified direction for the full value of the note.

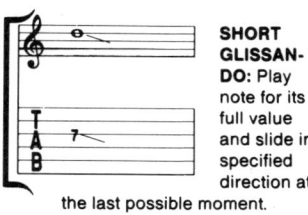

SHORT GLISSANDO: Play note for its full value and slide in specified direction at the last possible moment.

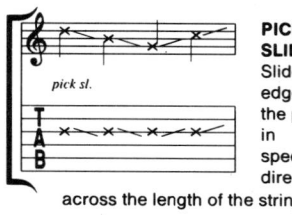

PICK SLIDE: Slide the edge of the pick in specified direction across the length of the string(s).

MUTED STRINGS: A percussive sound is made by laying the fret hand across all six strings while pick hand strikes specified area (low, mid, high strings).

PALM MUTE: The note or notes are muted by the palm of the pick hand by lightly touching the string(s) near the bridge.

TREMOLO PICKING: The note or notes are picked as fast as possible.

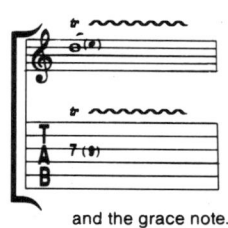

TRILL: Hammer on and pull off consecutively and as fast as possible between the original note and the grace note.

ACCENT: Notes or chords are to be played with added emphasis.

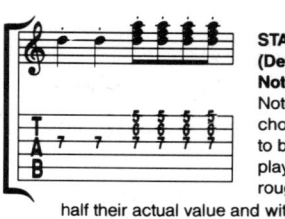

STACCATO (Detached Notes): Notes or chords are to be played roughly half their actual value and with separation.

DOWN STROKES AND UPSTROKES: Notes or chords are to be played with either a downstroke (⊓) or upstroke (∨) of the pick.

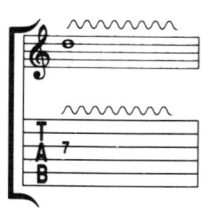

VIBRATO: The pitch of a note is varied by a rapid shaking of the fret hand finger, wrist, and forearm.